# THE NEW YORK BOTANICAL GARDEN COOKBOOK

*By Sharen Benenson*

*Edited by Jules Bond*

NY
BG

*Published by*
*The Council of The New York*
*Botanical Garden*

Library of Congress card number 81-70266
Printed in the U.S.A.

*Designed by Samuel N. Antupit*
*Creative coordination by Holland Vose Brigham*
*Printing supervision by Evan Konecky and*
*Konecky Associates*
*Book photography by Alan Rokach*
*Jacket photography by Bob Stern*

The New York Botanical Garden Cookbook
Box 8140V, The New York Botanical Garden
Bronx, New York 10458

# Contents

# THE
# NEW YORK
# BOTANICAL
# GARDEN

As President of The New York Botanical Garden, I have been deeply impressed by the scope and quality of the activities carried out by this institution. Its wide variety of programmatic activities, first rate scientific resources, and its impact on the local, national, and international communities rank it as a world class botanical and horticultural facility.

The Garden consists of two units: the original 250-acre Garden in the Bronx and the 1,950-acre Cary Arboretum, 70 miles north of the City at Millbrook, New York. The two units function as a single institution.

Most people know the Garden for the beauty of its landscapes and horticultural displays. However, some of our major functions such as research and education in the plant sciences are little known to the general public. The Garden is a treasury of scientific botanical information. The herbarium, a collection of preserved plants, contains over 4,300,000 specimens. It is one of the world's largest and most frequently consulted herbaria. The scientific activity at the Garden is in the forefront of exploring, analyzing, and classifying plants and in ecological and environmental research. The graduate training program, which prepares candidates for a doctorate in botany, is widely recognized for its excellence. The Garden also publishes seven scientific journals and a popular magazine, *Garden*. These help to report the results of our research around the world.

The Enid A. Haupt Conservatory, rededicated after extensive renovation on March 18, 1978,

*Almond*
**The Herball**

is a showcase for innovative interior floral design and for display of generic and geographical groupings of plants. One of the world's richest collections of tropical and subtropical ferns is now housed in it. In addition to this indoor display, there is a variety of other plant displays at both the Bronx and Cary campuses.

The Library of The New York Botanical Garden is one of the richest specialized collections in North America and serves a multitude of local, regional, and international needs. It is the only library in greater New York actively building a comprehensive collection of botanical and horticultural publications. It is composed of over 600,000 entries: books, journals, photographs, archives, manuscripts, and works of botanical art. Each year over 10,000 people come to the Garden to use this library for furthering studies of the plant world. In addition to fostering knowledge at home, it offers its services to research specialists abroad, particularly those in developing countries.

The Garden's important mission for the future is to use its resources in the best possible manner to foster botanical investigation, public education, public horticulture, the training of botanists and horticulturists, and the safeguarding of our environment. Our dedicated staff and volunteers look forward to this challenge. Through our combined efforts, lasting contributions will be made to the advancement of knowledge essential to human welfare and the enrichment of the lives of all mankind.
—DR. JAMES M. HESTER
*President*

*Lily*
Kreuterbuch (Lonitzer)

# Appetizers

# CHEDDAR CHEESE APPETIZER

1  lb. white, aged, sharp cheddar
   cheese
1  7-oz. jar pimientos
1  cup scallions (finely chopped)
½  cup mayonnaise
2  tsp. fresh lemon juice
1  tsp. finely minced fresh garlic
2  tbsp. Worcestershire sauce
¼  tsp. freshly ground black
   pepper

Use a meat grinder, if possible, or grate cheese on a grater, using coarse side. Add pimientos and scallions and blend together. Mix the mayonnaise with the rest of the ingredients and add to cheese mixture. Blend well. May be refrigerated if made well ahead of serving time, but be sure to remove from refrigerator and let come to room temperature before serving.

*Serves 20*
                                        —GERRY CALIENDO

# HOMEMADE "BOURSIN"

2  8-oz. packages of Philadelphia
   cream cheese
1  container whipped butter
1  tsp. oregano
½  tsp. each thyme, marjoram,
   basil, dill, garlic powder,
   Lowry's seasoned salt, Jane's
   Crazy Mixed-up salt, and some
   freshly ground pepper

Combine all ingredients, blend in food processor or blender. For a firmer mix, use plain butter. Can be frozen.

                                        —MRS. BURNHAM BOWDEN

# HUMMUS

Rub chick peas through a sieve, beat in tahini and lemon juice, a little at a time until smooth. Add garlic and salt and beat again until well blended and smooth. A food processor or electric blender will greatly simplify the preparation and produce a smoother dip. Put ingredients in the processor or blender and blend until smooth. When serving, sprinkle with paprika and parsley. Use as a dip or spread on toast fingers or crackers.

* Tahini is ground sesame seeds. It is a rather thick oil or a thin paste, available in all stores specializing in Greek and Middle Eastern food.
*Yields 2 cups*                —HANNAH M. RHODES

1   cup cooked chick peas
    (*canned may be used*)
*juice of 2 lemons*
3   cloves garlic, crushed
*salt to taste*
½   cup tahini*
1   tsp. paprika
1   tbsp. parsley, chopped

# FAVORITE DIP

Blend roquefort and cream cheese. Mix in the other ingredients. Serve at room temperature with crackers or corn chips. May be refrigerated in a covered jar as long as 2 weeks.
*Yields 2 pints*          —MRS. HENRY deF. BALDWIN

8-oz. cream cheese
4-oz. Roquefort cheese
⅓   cup diced flesh of cucumber
⅓   cup diced green pepper
¼–⅓ cup diced spring onion
1   tbsp. mayonnaise
dash of paprika

# SUMMER APPETIZER

4   large garden tomatoes
4   hard-boiled eggs
1   cup mayonnaise
4   leafy stems of basil

Core the tomatoes and cut a thin slice off the stem end if necessary to make them sit flat. Cut 6 slices down into the tomato from top to bottom leaving the bottom joined. Cut each egg in half and then cut each half in three slices. Cut the largest basil leaves in half lengthwise to make 24 strips. Put 2 tablespoons of mayonnaise in a small dish. Dip a slice of egg halfway into the mayonnaise, fold it in a sliver of basil, and insert it into a slit of a tomato. Continue until the tomatoes are filled. Top each tomato with a spoonful of the remaining mayonnaise. Chop the remaining basil and sprinkle it over the top.
*Serves 4*                    —MRS. HARDING BANCROFT

# RED CAVIAR MOUSSE

6-oz. red caviar
¼   cup chopped parsley
1   tbsp. grated onion
1   tsp. grated lemon peel
3   scallions, chopped
3   tbsp. diced, seeded cucumbers
2   cups sour cream
1   envelope gelatin
¼   cup hot water
1   cup whipping cream

Place the first 6 ingredients in a large bowl. Gently fold in the sour cream. Dissolve the gelatin in hot water and cool to room temperature. Beat the cream stiff, beating in the gelatin dissolved in the water. Immediately fold the whipped cream into the caviar mixture. Pour into a 6-cup mold and chill until set. This can be made the day ahead. Serve unmolded, with pumpernickle bread.
*Serves 30 people*          —BETTIE RODES BALDWIN

# SHRIMP SPREAD FOR CANAPÉS

Place shrimp, mayonnaise, Tabasco, onion juice, salt and pepper in blender—add enough cream until mixture has spreading consistency.

Spread on sesame seed wafers or place a dollop in artichoke bottoms.

*Yields 24 canapés* —MRS. GRAYSON L. KIRK

10 large cooked shrimp
¼ cup mayonnaise
3 shakes of Tabasco
1 tsp. onion juice
*salt and pepper*
*cream*


# HAM SQUARES

Blend all ingredients except egg whites. Fold egg whites into the mixture. Pour in a greased baking dish and bake at 350° for about 20 to 25 minutes until top is golden brown. Cut into small squares and serve hot.

*Hors d'oeuvres for 10* —MARY AMBROSE

1 tbsp. butter, softened
1 tbsp. unflavored breadcrumbs
1 tbsp. grated sharp cheese
½ cup sour cream
*pepper to taste*
¾ cup minced boiled ham
½ tsp. paprika
3 egg yolks, lightly beaten
3 egg whites, beaten stiff


# SAUSAGE BALLS

Mix above ingredients and roll in small balls. Bake 15 to 20 minutes at 350° in a shallow pan. Freezes well.

*Yields about 50 canapés* —MRS. LEWIS F. CAMP

1 lb. sausage meat
3 cups Bisquick
10-oz. sharp cheese, grated
*dash of red pepper (optional)*

# SALMON PÂTÉ

1  large can red salmon
8-oz. cream cheese, softened
1  tbsp. lemon juice
1  tbsp. horseradish, drained
1  tbsp. finely diced onion or
   scallion
¼  tsp. liquid smoke
½  cup chopped pecans or other
   nuts

Drain salmon well, remove skin and bones and mash with a fork. Blend in cream cheese and seasonings and mix thoroughly. Chill mixture until firm, form into a ball and roll in chopped nuts to coat completely. Store in refrigerator until ready to serve.
Serves 8–10
—EILEEN K. SCHOFIELD

# PIQUANT PATTIES

1  pkg. (8-oz.) cream cheese
2  tsp. drained prepared
   horseradish
2  tsp. finely chopped dill pickle
2  tsp. drained chopped capers
1  tsp. minced almonds
1  tsp. minced parsley
1  tsp. chopped chives
ground nuts and chopped parsley

Combine all ingredients and form into ½-inch balls. Roll in ground nuts and chopped parsley.
Serves 6
—MRS. BAYARD WALKER

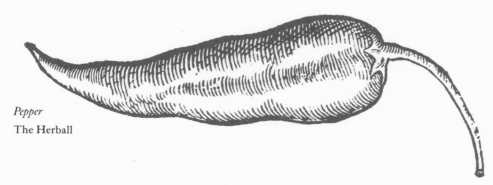

Pepper
The Herball

# CHEESE CROQUETTES

Work cheese with your hands until it begins to get soft. Add 1 tablespoon flour, egg, parsley, and salt; blend and shape the mixture in small croquettes or balls. Dredge in flour and fry in hot oil until golden brown.

You can also shape the cheese croquettes or balls around a pitted olive or a rolled anchovy filet.
*Yields 2 dozen hors d'oeuvres* —S. DORSEY SMITH

½ lb. mozzarella cheese
1 tbsp. flour
1 egg
1 tbsp. parsley, minced
salt to taste
flour
1 cup olive oil


# BLUE CHEESE DIP

Blend all ingredients, let stand for several hours before serving.

—BARBARA ROSENTHAL

1 cup mayonnaise
½ cup blue cheese
1 clove minced garlic
1 tbsp. onion
2 hard boiled eggs chopped
2 tbsp. pimiento
4 small sweet pickles chopped
1 tsp. capers
minced parsley
1 tsp. dry mustard
½ tsp. salt
4 drops Tabasco

*Marjoram*

*Our dantiest women doe put it to still amoung their other sweet hearbs, to make washing water.*
—PARKINSON'S HERBAL

# ZUCCHINI APPETIZERS

3   *cups thin sliced, unpared zucchini (about 4 small ones)*
1   *cup Bisquick*
½   *cup chopped onion or scallions*
½   *cup Parmesan cheese*
2   *tbsp. chopped parsley*
½   *tsp. salt*
½   *tsp. seasoned salt*
½   *tsp. dried oregano leaves*
1   *garlic clove, minced*
*dash of pepper*
½   *cup vegetable oil*
4   *eggs slightly beaten*

Mix all ingredients together. Spread in 13 × 9 × 2″ pan. Bake at 350° about ½ hour or until firm. Cut into small squares.

This can be frozen and then reheated for 7–10 minutes in a 400° oven.

*Hors d'oeuvres for 24*    —DOROTHY GREENLEE

# FRIED ANCHOVY BREAD

16   *slices of bread from a long loaf of French or Italian bread, cut ½ inch thick*
8   *thin slices of mozzarella cheese*
8   *anchovy filets*
1   *cup milk*
*flour*
2   *eggs, lightly beaten with 1 tbsp. of milk*
*olive oil for frying (about 1 cup)*
1   *small jar of canned pimiento*

Place a slice of cheese and one anchovy filet on each of 8 slices of bread. Put a few thin strips of pimiento on each. Cover with another slice of bread. Sprinkle these sandwiches on both sides with milk, then dredge in flour, dip in the egg and fry in oil until golden brown on both sides.

*Hors d'oeuvres for 8*    —AIMÉE JONES

# TINY CHEESE BISCUITS

Cream butter. Add cheese and blend until smooth. Add flour, salt, pepper and Rice Krispies. Drop from a teaspoon onto an ungreased baking sheet, and flatten with a fork. Bake 10 to 15 minutes at 350°. Serve warm or cold. These store well and may be reheated.

*Yields about 5 dozen*   —MRS. JOHN W. SANFORD

¼ *lb. butter*
1  *cup grated cheddar*
1  *cup sifted flour*
1  *cup Rice Krispies*
*pinch cayenne pepper*
*salt to taste*

# CHEESE STRAWS

Blend flour with cheese, salt and softened butter. Gradually add half milk and half ice water, just enough to make a stiff dough. Roll out ¼-inch thick. Cut in strips ¼-inch wide and about 4 to 5 inches long. Put on a baking sheet and bake at 400° for about 10 minutes until golden brown.

*Serves 6 to 8*   —MRS. LEWIS F. CAMP

2  *cups sifted flour*
2  *cups grated cheddar cheese,*
   *(or 1½ cups cheddar and*
   *½ cup Parmesan)*
1  *tsp. salt*
1½ *tbsp. butter*
*cold milk*
*ice water*

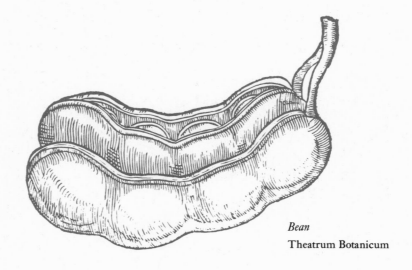

*Bean*
Theatrum Botanicum

# Soups

# CELERY AND ALMOND SOUP

2 tbsp. butter
4 cups (about 1 lb.) sliced
   celery
½ tsp. curry powder
2 cups chicken broth
1 tbsp. (heaping) minced
   parsley
milk
4 tbsp. slivered almonds

Cook butter, celery and curry over low heat about 10 minutes, stirring occasionally. Add broth and parsley. Bring to boil, cover and simmer 20 minutes. Liquefy in blender, adding enough milk to make 4 cups.

Heat and serve garnished with almonds.
*Serves 4*      —CONSTANCE E. STEVENS

# AJO BLANCO

1½ cups blanched almonds
5 cloves garlic
2–3 cups boiling water
1 cup salad oil
1 cup crushed ice
2 tsp. salt or to taste
green grapes to garnish

In a blender purée the almonds and garlic with 2 cups of boiling water. Add the oil while pureeing and more water if necessary. You may wish to use less garlic, but the literal translation of "ajo blanco" is "white garlic," and the flavor should be very strong. Chill the purée several hours and then taste it. Press it through a sieve if it seems too grainy. Add salt to taste and just before serving, whirl the purée in the blender again with the crushed ice. Serve in chilled glasses or bowls, garnished with peeled, seedless grapes. This soup is a favorite in Málaga, Spain, when the almonds are harvested.
*Serves 4*      —MONINA VON OPEL

# SORREL SOUP

Melt butter, chop fine parsley, lettuce, sorrel and onion. Put in pan with butter and cook until wilted. Add flour, stock, blend and simmer for 10 minutes. Beat egg yolks. Add cream. Combine with a little of the soup, add to the rest of the soup and heat. Do not boil. May be served hot or cold.

*Serves 8*
      —ALICE GREER &
     MRS. CHARLES BURLINGHAM

2 *tbsp. butter*
3 *sprigs parsley*
3 *leaves lettuce*
1 *medium onion*
2 *tbsp. flour*
1 *pint sorrel*
*nutmeg, salt, pepper*
2 *qts. stock (chicken or veal)*
*chervil or basil*
2 *egg yolks*
1 *cup cream*

# SQUASH SOUP

Cook the green or yellow peelings and the onion in one quart of broth until they are very soft. Mash or purée them and strain the liquid. Cook the flour in the butter without browning it. Stir in the squash mixture and the remaining quart of broth and simmer until thickened. Stir the egg and yolks and cream together. Remove hot soup from stove and quickly stir in the cream and yolks to blend.

*Serves 6*
     —MRS. JOHN E. LOCKWOOD

½ *lb. peelings from tender*
  *squash*
1 *onion, chopped*
2 *quarts broth*
4 *tbsp. butter*
2 *tbsp. flour*
2 *egg yolks*
½ *cup cream*
*salt and pepper to taste*

# WINTER SQUASH SOUP

1 small butternut squash
4 slices bacon
1 clove garlic, minced
1 onion, chopped
1 16-oz. can crushed tomatoes
2 cups beef broth
1 bay leaf
¼ cup minced fresh parsley
¼ tsp. dried basil
⅛ tsp. dried thyme
salt and pepper to taste
3 tbsp. dry sherry

Pare squash, remove seeds, cut into small cubes and set aside. In a skillet, cook bacon until crisp, drain on paper towels and crumble. Drain off all but 1 tablespoon fat from skillet, add garlic and onion and sauté for 5 minutes. Transfer garlic and onion to large saucepan, add squash, tomatoes, beef broth and seasonings. Cover saucepan and simmer for 30 minutes, or until squash is tender. Just before serving, remove bay leaf, stir in sherry and bacon pieces.

*Serves 4*
—EILEEN K. SCHOFIELD

# MUSHROOM VEGETABLE SOUP

¼ cup olive (or other) oil
2 green peppers, seeded and chopped
2 medium-sized zucchini (do not peel), chopped
1 lb. mushrooms, chopped
1 medium-sized onion, chopped
1 clove garlic, crushed
4 large ripe tomatoes, peeled and chopped
½ tsp. thyme
1 cup tomato juice
1 cup chicken broth

Gently sauté peppers, zucchini, mushrooms, onion, and garlic in oil until just soft. Add tomatoes, thyme, tomato juice and chicken broth. Bring to a boil, cover, reduce heat; simmer for 20–30 minutes. Season with salt to taste. Serve hot, over a little hot cooked rice in bottom of bowl or cup.

*Serves 4*
—LIZA FOSBURGH

# MINESTRONE

In a small saucepan, simmer bacon in water to cover for 5 minutes. Drain. Heat oil, butter and bacon in large saucepan or Dutch oven. Sauté onion, stirring occasionally, until deeply golden. Add carrot, celery, zucchini and cabbage. Cook and stir for 1 or 2 minutes, then add the tomatoes, salt and a few twists of pepper. Add the broth and water, which should cover the vegetables by 1 inch. Cover, lower heat, simmer at least 2 hours. Add cannellini beans the last 15 minutes of cooking. Soup should be thick. Add salt and pepper to taste. Serve with grated Parmesan cheese.

*Serves 8* —MRS. MICHAEL SLATER

¼  *lb. bacon, chopped*
⅓  *cup vegetable oil*
1  *tbsp. butter*
1  *large onion, thinly sliced (1 cup)*
1  *large carrot, cut in ¼ inch dice (½ cup)*
1  *large rib celery, cut in ¼ inch dice (½ cup)*
2  *medium-size zucchini, diced (2 cups)*
1  *cup shredded red cabbage*
⅓  *cup Italian plum tomatoes, with their juice, chopped*
½  *tsp. salt*
*freshly ground pepper*
1  *can condensed beef broth*
1½  *cups water*
1  *can (1 lb., 3 oz.) cannellini beans drained*
*grated Parmesan cheese*

*White Pepper*
The Herball

# MEAL IN A SOUP (A complete protein soup)

5    cups water
⅓    cup barley
⅓    cup brown rice
¼    cup lentils
¼    cup kidney beans
¼    cup pinto beans
¼    cup split peas
¼    cup elbow macaroni
1    stalk celery, chopped
1    carrot, chopped
1    onion, chopped
4    tomatoes, peeled and
     chopped
1    green pepper, chopped
salt, pepper, and oregano
     to taste

Bring water to boil. Rinse barley, rice, peas and beans and add with all other ingredients. Simmer approximately two hours, adding more water if necessary.

*Serves 4*

—REGINA BERENBACK

# AVOCADO SOUP

1    tbsp. butter
1    tbsp. flour
1½   cups hot chicken stock
1    ripe avocado
½    cup light cream
pinch of chili powder
pinch of white pepper
chives or parsley

Make a roux of the butter and flour; gradually add stock and cook over low heat for about 5 minutes. Scoop out avocado and mash until smooth or rub through a sieve or purée. Add avocado to stock and blend thoroughly. Add cream, chili powder, and white pepper. Season with salt to taste. Serve hot or cold, garnished with chopped chives or parsley; or a small amount of slightly salted whipped cream.

(Note: For a different taste, omit chili powder and add 1 teaspoon of curry powder.)

*Serves 2 to 3*

—LIZA FOSBURGH

# CALDO GALLEGO  Soup of Galicia (Northwestern Spain)

Cover peas with water, bring to a boil, drain and discard water. Meantime, cook vegetables, ham and sausage in olive oil until onion is tender. Remove and reserve 2–3 sausages. Add chick-peas, tomatoes and 4 quarts of water, also the herbs and seasonings. Simmer 3 hours or until the peas are tender. Purée in a food mill or blender. Reheat and add the reserved sausages, sliced, and the potatoes, diced. Cook 10 to 15 minutes, then add the spinach which has been thoroughly washed and chopped. Simmer for another 2 or 3 minutes and serve.

Serves 8
—FAITH H. McCURDY

1 ½  *pounds dried chick-peas*
1  *cup olive oil*
4  *medium onions, sliced*
4  *garlic cloves, crushed*
2  *cups cooked ham, minced*
1  *pound chorizo or Italian sausage*
2  *carrots*
1  *can tomatoes*
4  *quarts water*
2  *tsp. minced parsley*
1  *bay leaf, crushed*
*salt to taste*
*black pepper to taste*
4  *medium potatoes*
1  *pound spinach*

# CURRANT SOUP

Simmer the currants in the consommé for two hours. Strain and add a little hot liquid to the cream. Combine the cream and the consommé and season to taste with either sherry or curry powder. Serve with a dollop of whipped cream in each bowl and cracked pepper on top.

Serves 4
—MRS. DONALD STRAUS

4  *cans beef consommé*
½  *cup fresh currants*
2  *cups heavy cream*
*sherry or curry powder to taste*
*whipped cream for garnish*

# CREAM OF CARROT SOUP

4 tbsp. butter
1 lb. carrots
salt, pepper
½ onion, chopped
2 egg yolks
4 tbsp. flour
8 cups chicken broth
dash sugar
½ cup heavy cream

Peel the carrots. Reserve 2 of them for garnish and chop the rest. Melt the butter and add the flour to make a roux. Add the chopped onion and chopped carrots. Stir and cook for a few minutes. Remove from the heat and cool a little. Heat the chicken stock. Add the hot stock to the cooked roux, stirring. Let simmer for about 45 minutes. Purée the soup in a food processor or blender. Season to taste.

Julienne the two remaining carrots and cook them in boiling water with a pinch of sugar and salt added for just a few minutes, until they are barely tender. Refresh under cold water and reserve.

Both soup and garnish may be prepared ahead to this point and refrigerated. Right before serving, heat the soup to the boiling point. Mix the egg yolks with the cream. Add to the hot soup, stirring. Add the julienned carrots to heat. Serve immediately. Do not reboil the soup after adding the cream.

*Serves 8 to 10*

—PHYL MALLORY

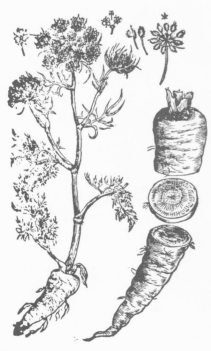

*Carrot*
De plantis epitome utilissima

# LAMB SHANK SOUP

Place the beans in a bowl and add cold water to cover about 2 inches above the beans. Soak overnight. Brown the lamb shanks on all sides in a heavy kettle. If there is any fat on the shanks, it is not necessary to add more fat to the kettle. Otherwise, brown them in one tablespoon of butter just so they don't stick. Pour off any fat that may have accumulated in the kettle. Drain the beans and add them to the kettle, along with salt to taste, the garlic, chicken broth and water. Cook partially covered, about one and one-half hours. Stir occasionally.

Add the vegetables and cook 30 minutes longer, stirring occasionally. Remove shanks and take the meat from the bone. Cut the meat into small pieces and return to the soup. Swirl in 2 tablespoons of butter and serve piping hot. May be made the day before. May also be frozen.

*Serves 6 to 8*                                 —MRS. C. E. ROCKWELL

| | |
|---|---|
| 1 | lb. dried lima beans |
| 1½ | lbs. lamb shanks (approximately) |
| 2 | tbsp. butter |
| 1 | clove garlic, crushed |
| 4 | cups chicken broth |
| 4 | cups water |
| ¾ | cup finely chopped onion |
| ¾ | cup finely diced carrots |
| ½ | cup finely chopped celery |

*The ordinary rosemary groweth in Spaine abundantly neare the seaside, the scent whereof is many times smelt by those in the shippes that passed by, many leagues off from the lande.*
*Rosemary is an herebe of as great use with us in these dayes, as anyother whatsoever, no onely for physicall, but for civill purposes: as all know, at weddings, funerals, etc. to bestow upon friends.*
                                                                        —PARKINSON'S HERBAL

# MADRILENE

3 to 4 ripe tomatoes

4    scallions, pared, chopped

2    egg whites and their
      crushed shells

2    tbsp. tarragon vinegar

2    tbsp. tomato paste

4½  cups chicken broth

1    envelope unflavored gelatin

1    tsp. tarragon

salt to taste

Cut up tomatoes, retaining their skin but removing seeds and hard parts. Put them in a large bowl. Add scallions, egg whites and crushed shells, tarragon vinegar, and tomato paste. Add 1 cup cold chicken broth, having first moistened and dissolved gelatin in a little of the broth. Add this too, also the dried tarragon. Heat remaining chicken broth, add hot broth to the mixture. (Always skim fat off the canned broth.) Place this mixture in a pot, bring to a boil, then simmer over very low heat, covered, without touching, for 15 minutes. Then strain contents through a sieve lined with a double cheesecloth. Do not press. Chill for 2 hours or more.

*Serves 4*       —MRS. JOHN E. PARSONS

Note: This is lots of fun as the soup comes out ruby-crystal clear and well flavored. (Canned Madrilene is horrible.)

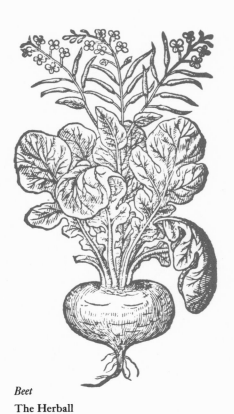

*Beet*
The Herball

# CHILLED CREAM OF MUSHROOM SOUP

Sauté mushrooms in butter until soft. Put chicken broth in a saucepan, add celery, onion and mushrooms and simmer for half an hour. Pour soup in a blender, purée until very smooth, season with salt and pepper. Blend cream with egg yolks and stir into soup. Return soup to pan, bring to a bare simmer, heat for 2 minutes. Chill for several hours.
*Serves 4 to 6*                    —ELIZABETH CORNING

¼ *lb. mushrooms, chopped*
1 *tbsp. butter*
4 *cups chicken broth*
1 *rib celery, chopped*
1 *small onion, chopped*
¼ *cup heavy cream*
2 *egg yolks, beaten*
*salt and pepper to taste*

# ICED BORSCHT

Chill first five ingredients. Place in a blender with crushed ice and blend 30 seconds or until smooth. Season to taste. Pour into bowls or goblets and top with sour cream.
*Serves 4*                    —MRS. ERASTUS CORNING

¾ *cup rich chicken broth (it should jell)*
1 *cup sour cream*
1 *slice of lemon, peeled and seeded*
1 *small onion, chopped*
1 *cup beets, cooked and diced*
1 *cup crushed ice*
*salt and Tabasco sauce*
*sour cream to garnish*

# Eggs & Cheese

# SPINACH QUICHE

1 unbaked pie shell
8-oz. Swiss cheese
10-oz. fresh spinach
1 onion
¼ cup raisins
3 eggs
1 cup milk
salt
Cayenne pepper and nutmeg

Shred the cheese. Cook the spinach in boiling water for 3 minutes; drain, squeeze dry, and chop it. You may substitute a package of thawed, frozen spinach. Mince the onion. Sprinkle ¾ of the cheese over the bottom of the pie shell. Distribute the spinach, onion, and raisins evenly over it. Beat the eggs, milk, salt, and pepper together and pour them gently into the shell. Sprinkle on the remaining cheese and bake at 350° for 45 minutes or until a tester comes out clean.
*Serves 6*

—CHARLOTTE HENKEN

Commentarii

# CRABMEAT QUICHE

1   unbaked 9-inch pie shell
1   7½-oz. can crabmeat
1   cup grated Swiss cheese
2   scallions, finely chopped
3   eggs
1   cup light cream
¼   tsp. dry mustard
⅛   tsp. mace
grated rind of ½ lemon
salt and pepper to taste
¼   cup slivered almonds (optional)

Drain crabmeat well and separate into small pieces. Spread cheese over bottom of pie shell, put crabmeat on top and sprinkle with scallions. Beat eggs, add cream and seasonings, and blend well. Pour mixture carefully over crabmeat and cheese. Sprinkle almonds on top, if desired. Bake at 375° for 35–40 minutes until well browned and a knife inserted near center comes out clean. Let cool 10 minutes before slicing. Leftovers are very good served cold.

*Serves 6*          —EILEEN K. SCHOFIELD

Hortus Sanitatis

# EASY CRAB AND EGG LUNCHEON DISH

6   hard cooked eggs
2   tbsp. butter
2   tbsp. flour
½   tsp. salt
1   cup half and half
⅓   cup sherry
½   cup sharp cheddar cheese, grated
1   cup crabmeat, fresh or canned

Peel and chop eggs coarsely and divide among 4 ramekins. In a heavy pan over low heat, stir the flour and salt into the butter and then cook three minutes, but do not brown. Remove from heat and stir in half and half and sherry. Return to heat and cook, stirring until thickened and starting to boil. Reduce heat and stir in all but 1 tablespoon cheese. When cheese has melted, stir in crabmeat. Divide equally among ramekins, top with remaining cheese, and bake at 350° for 15 minutes.

*Serves 4*                                    —PENNY McKOWN

De tuenda bona valetudine

## BAKED EGGS

8   slices bacon
½   lb. mushrooms
1   clove garlic
1   tbsp. white wine
1   tbsp. wheat germ
8   eggs

Cook bacon until not quite crisp. While it is still warm, curl one slice to line the walls of each lightly creased muffin cup. Discard most of the fat from the bacon pan. Dice the mushrooms and garlic and cook them quickly in the remaining fat. Just before they are done, add the wine and stir until it evaporates. Divide the mushrooms among the muffin cups and spread the mixture evenly over the bottom of each. Break an egg into each cup. Sprinkle the wheat germ on top. Bake at 350° for 15 minutes.
*Yields 8 eggs*
                              —LIZA FOSBURGH

## RED EGGS

2   eggs
3   slices onion
butter
2   tbsp. tomato catsup
2   tbsp. dry sherry
1   tsp. Worcestershire sauce
dash Tabasco sauce

Break eggs into a buttered baking dish and bake at 350° for 10 minutes or in a microwave oven until set. In a saucepan, wilt the onion in a little butter. Add the other ingredients and boil up once. Pour over the eggs.
*Serves 1*
                              —MRS. THOMAS H. CHOATE

# EGG
# RISSOLES

5   eggs
enriched béchamel sauce *(see below)*
½   tsp. curry powder
salt, pepper, flour
1   cup bread crumbs, approximately

Hard boil four of the eggs. Chop them fine and mix with enough béchamel sauce to stick them together. Season with salt, pepper and curry. Form the mixture into soup-spoon-size croquettes. Roll in flour to coat. Beat the fifth egg and dip the croquettes in it and then into the crumbs. Let stand 15 minutes to set. Fry in hot fat until browned. Serve hot.

Enriched Béchamel Sauce

3   tbsp. butter
3   tbsp. flour
1   cup milk
1   egg yolk
salt and pepper

In a heavy saucepan cook the butter and flour together 3 or 4 minutes without browning. Remove from heat and slowly stir in the milk. Return to heat and stir until sauce is thick and smooth. Remove from heat and stir in salt and pepper and the egg yolk. Sauce should be hot enough to cook the one yolk.

Thin the left-over sauce with cream, season with more fresh-ground pepper, reheat and serve at the side of the rissoles.

*Serves 2*                                    —MRS. WINSTON HAGEN

1½  tbsp. butter
2½  tbsp. flour
1½  cups milk
1    cup cream
1    lb. mushrooms
1    small onion
butter or oil
1    tbsp. chopped parsley
1    tsp. lemon juice
salt and pepper
5    eggs

# MUSHROOM SOUFFLÉ

Cook the butter and flour together 2 or 3 minutes without browning. Beat in the milk and cream and continue cooking until thick and smooth. Mince the onion and mushrooms and cook them in a little butter or oil for 5 minutes. Scrape them into the saucepan and stir. Stir in the parsley, lemon juice, salt and pepper. Beat in the egg yolks one at a time. Set the mixture aside to cool while you whip the egg whites stiff. Fold the mushroom mixture into the whites. Fill a buttered soufflé dish ⅔ full and place in the center of a 400° oven. Reduce the heat to 375° and bake 50 to 60 minutes until a knife inserted in the center or side comes out clean and the soufflé is beautifully browned.

*Serves 4 or 6*

—MRS. LAWRENCE McKEEVER MILLER

# TORTILLA

Spanish Potato and Onion
Omelet

1   cup + 2 tbsp. olive oil
2   medium potatoes, peeled and sliced into ⅛
    inch thick rounds
1   clove garlic (optional)
1   cup onions, chopped
½   cup green pepper, chopped
1   tbsp. pimientos
1   tbsp. salt
pepper
6   eggs

In a heavy 10–12 inch skillet, heat 1 cup olive oil over high heat until hot but not smoking. Add potatoes (and chopped garlic); coat well with oil. Reduce heat to moderate and cook for 8–10 minutes turning occasionally; then stir in onions and peppers, salt and pepper. Continue cooking over moderate heat for approximately 10 minutes until potatoes are tender and golden brown. Drain excess oil in colander. Beat eggs until frothy. Stir in the potato mixture. Heat the 2 tablespoons oil in a heavy 8-inch skillet. Pour in omelet mixture and cook over moderate heat for 2 minutes. Turn omelet onto plate and slide back into pan. Cook for 3 minutes to brown. Repeat turning if necessary to brown, or brown the bottom and then run under broiler to brown the top. Add previously fried chopped chorizo or other sausage if desired.

*Serves 2–3*                    —FAITH H. McCURDY

1    eggplant
6    hard boiled eggs
1    lb. mozzarella cheese
1    can tomato paste
1    tbsp. Parmesan cheese
salt and pepper to taste

# TORTONI DI MELANZANA ALLA PARMAGIANA

Slice an eggplant and prepare it for frying. Fry slices until tender in oil. Line a baking dish with the fried eggplant. Make a layer of hard boiled eggs cut in pieces as large as your thumb, ½-inch square pieces of cheese and tomato paste. Cover with eggplant and then add another layer of egg, cheese and tomato paste. Put a layer of eggplant over the top and cover lightly with grated parmesan. Bake until just hot.

*Serves 4 as a main dish*                    —H. B. POST

½    lb. shredded Swiss cheese
¼    cup dry white wine
3    anchovy filets, mashed
1    egg, lightly beaten
1    tbsp. pitted olives, chopped
1    tsp. pimiento, chopped
salt and pepper to taste
4    toasted English muffins

# CHEESE TOAST

Cut cheese and wine in a saucepan, melt over low heat and blend well, until thick and creamy. Add anchovy filets, egg, olives and pimiento, stir until well blended. Spread toasted muffins with the mixture, place them on a baking sheet and brown in a hot oven or under the broiler.

*Yields 8 pieces*                    —DONNA STEVENSON

De tuenda bona valetudine

# BAKED STUFFED TOMATOES

4 large, ripe, garden tomatoes
4 slices French bread
butter
1 cup grated cheddar cheese or 8 thin slices
4 eggs
1 tbsp. minced fresh herbs
salt and pepper
1½ cups fresh corn kernels
4 slices bacon

Remove the cores and seeds and hollow out the tomatoes. Butter each slice of French bread and place it, butter-side-down in an individual glass baking dish. Top each slice of bread with 2 tablespoons grated cheese or 1 slice. Set the tomato cups on the cheese. Break an egg into each tomato. Sprinkle in the herbs, salt, and pepper. Fill the tomatoes with corn or with leftover cooked vegetables. Top with the remaining cheese and a cross of bacon strips. Bake at 350° for 40 minutes.

*Serves 4*                    —MRS. PERCY L. DOUGLAS

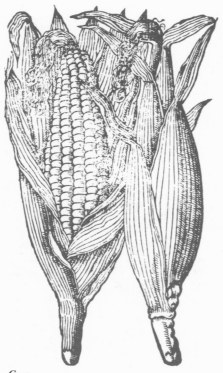

*Corn*
The Herball

2 cups quick grits
8 cups water
1 tbsp. salt
10-oz. shredded sharp cheddar cheese
1 or 2 cloves garlic, minced
¼ lb. butter, cut in pieces
4 egg yolks, beaten to light yellow
4 egg whites, beaten stiff

# GRITS SOUFFLÉ

Cook grits in water with salt according to package directions. Stirring until each is thoroughly incorporated, add garlic, cheese in three additions, butter and egg yolks. Fold in egg whites when mixture is lukewarm.

Bake at 350° 45 minutes in a wide greased casserole. This will puff and brown beautifully and is excellent as part of a buffet supper. It tastes just as good after it falls, and it can be reheated.
*Serves 12*                    —MRS. HAROLD C. RIKER

*Mint*

*Applied with salt, it is a safe medicine for the byting of a mad dogge.*

*Aristotle and others in the ancient times forbade mints to be used of Soldiers in the time of warre, because they thought it did so much incite to venery that it tooke away, or at least abated their animosity or courage to fight.*

*And some againe, that it is the juyce of mints be put into milke wherecome cheese.*

—PARKINSON'S HERBAL

# Fish & Shellfish

# BAKED CRABMEAT

1   lb. cooked crabmeat
¼   cup sherry
7   tbsp. butter
3   tbsp. flour
1   cup heavy cream
1   cup milk
4   hard boiled eggs
salt and pepper
¼   tsp. cayenne
½   tsp. dry mustard
1   cup toasted bread crumbs

Pick over the crabmeat, sprinkle it with sherry, and let soak a few minutes. Cook the flour for 3 or 4 minutes without browning it in 3 tablespoons of the butter. Slowly stir in the heated milk and cream and cook and stir until thickened and smooth. Stir in the sieved egg yolks and chopped egg whites. Mix the seasonings, moisten them with a little of the sauce, and then incorporate them in the sauce. Fold in the crabmeat and pour the mixture into a buttered six-cup baking dish or eight ramekins. Top with the bread crumbs and the remaining butter, melted. Bake at 375° about 15 minutes until sizzling hot and lightly browned.

*Serves 8*      —PHYL MALLOY

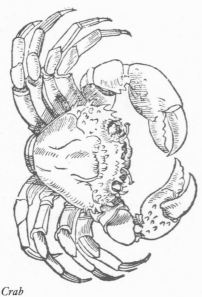

*Crab*
De medicinali materia

1   *pound small shrimp, shelled, and cut in half
    lengthwise*
¾   *pound feta cheese, crumbled in ½–1" pieces*
3   *tomatoes cut in ¾" chunks*
1   *small bunch dill, chopped*
1   *small clove garlic, cut in slivers*
*salt and fresh ground pepper*
½   *cup olive oil*

# GREEK SHRIMP

Put the first four ingredients in a wide, shallow baking dish so that they are not more than 2½" deep and evenly distributed. Sprinkle the garlic and about 1 teaspoon of salt over the top and grind on fresh pepper. Pour the olive oil evenly over all.

Bake 30–45 minutes in a 350° oven turning all ingredients over gently after 20 minutes. The dish is done when all the shrimp are pink and the feta on top is lightly browned. Serve with rice.

*Serves 6*                    —JAMES BENENSON, JR.

# NEW ORLEANS BAR-B-QUE SHRIMP WITH ROSEMARY

2   pounds large raw shrimp in the shell
3   sticks of butter
2   lemons
4   tbsp. Worcestershire sauce
2   tbsp. rosemary leaves
Tabasco to taste (it's best HOT)

Place raw shrimp one layer deep in a large baking dish. Melt butter in a saucepan and add all the seasonings. Juice one lemon and slice the second lemon, and throw it all in and simmer for 10–15 minutes. Pour the butter sauce over the shrimp and bake in a HOT oven (450°–500°) about 10 minutes or until the shrimp turn pink. Serve in the baking dish, peel and eat with fingers.

Serves 4 to 6       —HOLLAND VOSE

# SHRIMPS À LA HEISKELL

1   lb. shrimp with shells
small amount of butter
2   tsp. vermouth (dry)
herbs to taste (we use tarragon, basil or dill)

When butter has melted, place shrimp with vermouth, etc. in pan to cook, turning frequently until done.

Serve as is with large finger bowls with warm water. (Messy, but good.)

Serves 2       —MRS. ANDREW HEISKELL

1    can tomato soup

8-oz. cream cheese

1    cup mayonnaise

½    lb. fresh, cooked shrimp or 1 1-lb. can tiny
     shrimp, drained

⅓    cup minced onion

⅓    cup minced celery

1½   envelopes gelatine (1½ tbsp.)

¼    cup white wine

¼    cup water

lemon juice, salt, cayenne pepper


In a food processor, combine soup, cream
cheese, and mayonnaise. Add cooked shrimp and
chop coarsely. (If tiny canned shrimp are used,
don't chop them.) Turn mixture out into a
bowl and stir in the onion and celery. Dissolve
the gelatine in the water and wine and stir it into
the mixture. Season to taste with lemon juice, salt,
and cayenne. Pour into a lightly oiled 8-cup mold
or 8 individual molds and chill several hours until
set.

*Serves 8*                     —MRS. JOHN W. SANFORD

# SHRIMP MOLD

*Pepper*
Kreuterbuch (Lonitzer)

# CURRIED MUSSELS

1   very small clove garlic, *minced*
2–3 dashes cayenne pepper, or to taste
1   tsp. curry powder
1   cup heavy cream
1   quart very small mussels, well scrubbed

Sprinkle the garlic, pepper, and curry powder in a large heavy skillet and heat. When skillet is hot, slowly stir in cream. (Wait till you smell the curry toasting, but do not burn the garlic.) When cream begins to boil, add the mussels and continue to stir over high heat until mussels open. As they do, divide them between two warm soup plates. When all have been removed, continue boiling sauce to reduce it slightly. Pour sauce over mussels. This is a meal for two served with a salad and bread. Poured over hot, buttered pasta, it serves 4.

*Serves 2*                         —MARY HOMANS

Commentarii

4   doz. large mussels
3   tbsp. olive oil
1   large onion, minced
1   large carrot, peeled, minced
2   small potatoes, peeled, diced
1   cup minced heart of celery (white part)
2   large cloves garlic, crushed
2   tomatoes, peeled, seeded, chopped
1   tsp. lemon juice
1   tsp. sugar
a few threads of saffron
pepper to taste
2   tbsp. parsley, minced

# MUSSEL STEW

Wash mussels and scrub with a stiff brush. Place mussels with ¼ cup water in a saucepan, cover and cook over high heat for 3 or 4 minutes until shells open. Remove from fire, discard unopened mussels. Take mussels out of shells and reserve. Strain juice through several layers of cheesecloth and reserve.

Heat oil in a skillet. Sauté onion until light golden, add carrots, potatoes, celery, sauté 2 minutes longer. Add garlic, tomatoes, lemon juice, sugar, saffron and pepper; mix well. Add 1 cup of mussel juice, cover and simmer for 25 minutes. Stir occasionally, add more mussel juice if too dry. Add mussels, salt if needed, heat through, sprinkle with parsley and serve.

*Serves 4*                    —NANCY HECKSHIRE

# LOBSTER STEW

2 live 2-lb. lobsters
4 tbsp. butter
6 cups light cream
1 cup chicken broth
1 tsp. paprika
pinch of cayenne pepper
salt and pepper to taste
3 tbsp. sherry wine

Plunge lobsters in boiling water, boil for 8 to 9 minutes after water startes to boil again. Remove tail and claw meat, also tomalley and coral, if any. Do this over a pan to catch and save all the lobster juices. Cut meat into bite size pieces, put together with lobster juices and tomalley in a saucepan. Add butter and simmer until butter melts and all lobster pieces are well coated. Heat cream in a double boiler to the scalding point, add lobster and all juuices, chicken broth, paprika, cayenne, salt and pepper. Stir well and heat through. Remove from heat, cool and refrigerate for 24 hours. Before serving, heat in double boiler and stir in sherry.

*Serves 4*                                    —MARY AMBROSE

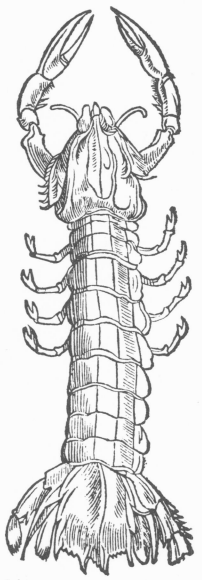

*Lobster*
De medicinali materia

½   *lb. diced salt pork*

2   *cups sliced onions*

5½  *cups diced potatoes*

6   *cups water*

2   *bottles clam juice*

3   *lbs. fillet of haddock or cod or other white fish—fresh or frozen*

1   *cup chopped clams—fresh if available—or 2 cans chopped clams*

½   *lb. crabmeat or small shrimp*

1½  *qts. milk*

*thyme*

*salt and pepper*

*parsley, chopped*

*flour and butter*

*soda crackers*

# CLAM AND FISH CHOWDER

Try out salt pork until brown, remove pieces and reserve. Add onions and sauté. Add potatoes, water and clam juice, cook about 5 minutes, then add fish fillets and cook until flaky. Add chopped clams, crabmeat or shrimp. Season with salt and ground pepper, thyme and parsley. This can be done ahead and refrigerated (even overnight).

Reheat, add milk and heat. If a thicker soup is desired, add flour and butter kneaded together.

Serve in heated bowls with soda crackers.

*Serves 12*
                  —FAITH H. McCURDY

# THIMBLE ISLANDS CLAM CHOWDER

1   dozen littleneck clams
2"  cube salt pork or smoked bacon
1   large yellow onion
1   baking potato, peeled
1   large summer tomato or 12–15 cherry tomatoes
2–3 cups water
salt and pepper

Cube the salt pork in ¼"–⅜" cubes. Cook in a heavy saucepan over low heat to extract most of the fat. Meanwhile, chop the onion in ½-inch pieces and the potato in slightly smaller cubes. Stir the onion into the rendered fat, cover the pot and continue cooking to just barely soften the onion. Stir in the potato to mix. Add water to cover the vegetables by about ½ inch. Cover the pot and raise heat to high. As soon as water begins to boil put the washed clams, hinge side down, on top of the vegetables. Simmer till clams open, lift them out with a slotted spoon, and put the tomato, cut in ¾-inch cubes, in the pot. Cover and continue to simmer while you remove the clams from the shells. As soon as you have them all out, stir them into the simmering chowder. Add fresh ground pepper and serve. Don't cook any longer or clams will toughen and vegetables will get mushy.

This recipe was given to me by the ferryboat captain in the Thimble Islands off Branford, Connecticut. His family has been preparing it since colonial times.

*Serves 2*                           —SHAREN BENENSON

*1   pie shell (double)*
*10  sea clams or 2 pts. quahogs*
*3-oz. salt pork, minced*
*⅔   cup onion*
*1   cup bread or cracker crumbs*
*½   pint cream*
*fresh-ground pepper*

# CLAM PIE

Grind clams (or chop fine). Fry salt pork and onion lightly. Add clams to pork mixture and cook until clams shrink a little.

Remove from fire and add crumbs, salt, pepper and cream. Put in pie shell, dot with butter. Cover with top crust and brush it with milk. Bake at 375° for 35 to 45 minutes.

*Serves 6*                              —MRS. GRAYSON L. KIRK

*24  oysters on the half-shell*
*3   tbsp. anchovy paste*
*1   tsp. onion juice*
*1   tsp. lemon juice*
*Tabasco sauce*
*3   tbsp. Parmesan cheese*

# BAKED OYSTERS

Mix the anchovy paste, onion and lemon juices and Tabasco to taste. Put a drop on each oyster. Sprinkle on Parmesan and run the oysters under the broiler until they are hot through and the cheese is browned. Serve immediately. This is a very satisfying low-calorie lunch served with a salad.

*Serves 4*                              —MRS. CLARENCE STANLEY

# CREAMED OYSTERS

2 dozen oysters with their liquor
6 tbsp. butter
4 rounded tbsp. flour
2 cups milk
2 cups cream
4 small carrots
4 small white onions
1 white turnip
4 hearts of celery with leaves
chopped parsley
salt and pepper
8 slices toast

Cook the flour in 2 tablespoons of butter for 3 or 4 minutes without browning it. Remove from heat and stir in the scalded milk. Cook and stir until the mixture is thick and smooth and then stir in the cream. Chop the vegetables in small dice and cook slowly in 2 tablespoons of the butter until they are soft. Scrape them into the cream sauce and simmer very gently. Add the oyster liquor to the cream sauce and cook the oysters in the remaining tablespoon of butter until their edges curl. Stir them into the hot sauce and serve immediately on toast garnished with parsley.

*Serves 6 to 8*

—MRS. WINSTON HAGEN

1 lb. bay scallops
¼ cup flour
½ tsp. salt
pinch pepper
¼ cup butter + 2 tbsp.
2 tbsp. lemon juice
1 tsp. grated lemon rind
2 tbsp. minced parsley

# BAY SCALLOPS SUPREME

Shake the scallops in a bag with the flour, salt, and pepper. Heat the ¼ cup butter very hot and sauté the scallops about 3 minutes until lightly browned. Do not overcook. Remove the scallops to a hot dish using a slotted spoon. Quickly stir the remaining 2 tablespoons butter, juice, rind, and half the parsley into the pan and boil up. Pour the sauce over the scallops and dust with the remaining parsley before serving.

*Serves 3 or 4*                    —ELEANOR ISDALE

*Cabbage or Colewort*

*They are much commended being eaten to keepe one from surfetting as from being drunk with much wine, by restaining the vapours that else would intoxicate the braine, or being drunke, will disperse the vapours and make them quickly rise sober againe . . . apply the juyce thereof, to the temples of them that had paines in their heads caused by drunkenesse. For as they say, there is such an antiphathy or enmity betweene the vine and the colewort, that the one will die where the other groweth.*                    —PARKINSON'S HERBAL

# SAUTÉED
# BAY
# SCALLOPS

1   lb. scallops
¼   cup dry vermouth
1   small clove garlic, minced
salt and pepper to taste
fine dry white breadcrumbs
butter

Put scallops in a bowl, add vermouth, garlic, salt and pepper, mix well and let stand for one hour. Drain scallops, pat dry with paper towels. Roll the scallops in breadcrumbs. Heat butter in a heavy skillet—the butter should be about ¼ inch deep. Shake excess breadcrumbs off scallops and sauté quickly over fairly high heat for no more than 2 or 3 minutes, until golden brown. Remove with a slotted spoon and serve with lemon wedges.

*Note:* The scallops are not really breaded; the crumbs will not adhere to the scallops. They will, however, have soaked up excess liquid, if any, and provide a crunchy contrast to the tender shellfish. Sea scallops could be used instead of bay scallops. Cut them into two or three pieces before marinating.

*Serves 2 to 3*

—DAVID PACE

4   small red snapper fillets
6   tbsp. butter
juice of 1 lemon
4   fresh ripe tomatoes
3   tbsp. dry bread crumbs
paprika and pepper to taste
1–2  tbsp. Parmesan cheese

## RED SNAPPER FILLETS

Melt butter in a small saucepan and use some to butter a baking dish big enough to hold the fillets in one layer. Add the lemon juice to the remaining butter and let it simmer while you assemble the remaining ingredients.

Slice the tomatoes thinly and layer them in the baking dish with the bread crumbs. Place filets on top and season with pepper and paprika. Pour butter and lemon juice evenly over fish, sprinkle with cheese, and bake 10 minutes at 500°.

*Serves 4*                          —MRS. ROBERT G. BERRY

1   pair shad roe
2   shad fillets
2   medium onions, sliced and separated into rings
4   tbsp. butter, cut in little pieces

## BAKED SHAD AND ROE

Poach roe very gently in salted water for 5 minutes. Lay sides of shad skin-side down in a buttered baking dish. Lay the roe, divided in half, down the center. Scatter the onions and butter over all. Cover dish tightly with aluminum foil and bake 30 minutes at 350°.

*Serves 4*                          —JUDITH BECKWITH

# BROILED MACKEREL

1 medium mackerel
2 tbsp. olive oil
1 large clove garlic, crushed
1 tbsp. parsley, minced
½ tsp. basil
½ tsp. oregano
¼ tsp. rosemary, crushed
2 tbsp. grated onion
pinch of cayenne pepper (opt.)
1 tsp. Dijon mustard
2 tbsp. lemon juice
salt and pepper to taste

Have mackerel cleaned, split and boned. Blend all other ingredients. Put mackerel, skin side down, on a broiler rack. Brush with the herb mixture, let stand for one hour. Heat broiler, broil fish for about 10 minutes until done and browned. Brush once or twice with the mixture while broiling.

*Serves 2*
—DAVID PACE

2    bluefish fillets, about ½ lb. each
white vinegar
1    tbsp. parsley, chopped
1½  tbsp. onion, grated
1    large tomato, peeled, seeded, diced
1    small green pepper, seeded, diced
1    tsp. Dijon mustard
2    tbsp. cocktail sauce
1    tsp. prepared horseradish
2    tbsp. dry white wine
salt and pepper to taste
Tabasco sauce to taste (opt.)
green chili peppers to taste (opt.)
1    tbsp. white vinegar

# BLUEFISH SEVICHE

Cut fillets into cubes or strips, cover with vinegar and marinate 2 to 4 hours. Drain. Mix with diced tomato, pepper, onion, and parsley, season with salt and pepper. Blend 1 tablespoon vinegar, wine, mustard and add to fish with all other ingredients. Chill well before serving.

*Note:* Other fish, such as flounder, bass, snapper, etc. can be prepared the same way.

*Serves 6 to 8*                    —NANCY HECKSHIRE

*Pepper*
The Herball

59.

# FISH ROLATINI

3 fillets of sole or other white fish
2 tsp. lemon juice
1 tsp. minced garlic
1 tbsp. minced oregano or fresh herb of your choice
2 tbsp. grated Parmesan
fresh-ground pepper
¼ cup butter

Lay fish flat and sprinkle with lemon juice on both sides. Cut fillet crossways into 2-inch wide strips. Mince together the garlic, herb, 1 tablespoon of cheese and pepper. Sprinkle over the fish. Roll fish and place in a buttered baking dish so that the rolls touch and hold each other in place. Sprinkle on the remaining tablespoon of cheese. Melt the remaining butter and pour over all. Bake at 375° for 20 minutes or until fish flakes.

*Serves 2 to 4*                    —ANN ISAACSON

De medicinali materia

2  cups mashed potatoes or 3 medium sized
   potatoes, boiled and diced
1½ lbs. fresh or frozen fish fillets
2  tbsp. butter
2  tbsp. flour
2  tbsp. lemon juice
1  cup chicken broth
salt
1  tbsp. chopped chives
1  tbsp. grated lemon rind

Put potatoes in the bottom of a shallow buttered baking dish. Place fish on top. Make sauce by melting butter, blending in flour and adding lemon juice, chicken broth, salt and pepper. Pour over fish and potatoes. Sprinkle top with chives and lemon rind. Bake in 350° oven 20 to 25 minutes.

*Serves 4*
—MARIANNE BLOCK

*Sambucus Elder*

*If you shall put some of the fresh flowers of Elders into a bagge, letting it hang in a vessel of wine, when it is made new, and beginneth to boyle the bagge being a little pressed every evening, for a seavon night to gether, giveth the wine a very good rellish and a smell like muscadine (and will doe little lesse to ale or beer).*
—PARKINSON'S HERBAL

# BAKED HADDOCK WITH CELERY DRESSING

2   fillets of haddock (1½ lbs. each)
salt and pepper
½   cup minced celery stalks and leaves
⅓   cup minced onion
3   tbsp. butter
4   leaves sage, minced (1 tsp. dried)
⅓   cup minced parsley
1   cup soft bread crumbs
½   cup milk
½   cup cream

Place one fillet in a buttered oblong or oval baking dish. Sprinkle with salt and pepper. Wilt the celery and onion in the butter. Remove from heat and toss with the parsley, sage, crumbs, and salt and pepper to taste. Add enough milk to moisten the dressing and spread it on the fillet. Cover with the second fillet. Pour over the remaining milk and cream and bake at 350° for 30 minutes or until fish flakes.

*Serves 4 to 6*

—MRS. LAWRENCE McKEEVER MILLER

*Sage*
I discorsi

2 lbs., approximately, fresh salmon—center cut
½ cup salt
¼ cup sugar
20 coarsely ground white peppercorns
2-oz. chopped dill (about 4 bunches)

# GRAVLAX

Cut salmon into fillets. Do not remove skin. Wipe fish dry with a paper towel; do not rinse. Rub the fish with the salt mixed with sugar. Sprinkle part of the salt mixture and some dill in a deep enamel or stainless baking dish. Place one piece of salmon, skin side down, in the dish and sprinkle generously with dill, crushed peppercorns and salt mixture. Cover with second piece of fish, skin side up. Sprinkle with remaining salt mixture. Cover with aluminum foil and a light weight (a chopping board). Refrigerate for at least 1 to 2 days, turning salmon around every day. The gravlax will keep for 3 weeks in the refrigerator.

To serve, cut in thin slices free from skin.
*Serves 6*

Gravlax Sauce

3 tbsp. oil
1 tbsp. red wine vinegar
1 tbsp. sugar
dash of salt
pinch of white pepper
2 or 3 tbsp. prepared mustard
2 or 3 tbsp. finely chopped dill

Beat together all ingredients except dill. Add dill or serve it from a separate bowl.

—ERIC FRIBERG

*Poultry & Game Birds*

# BROILED MARINATED CHICKEN

3 2-lb. broiler chickens
½ cup olive oil
1 lemon + juice of 2 lemons
3 cloves garlic
3 tsp. sweet paprika
½ tsp. pepper
1 tsp. salt
½ cup white wine
watercress

Split the chickens in half and rub with olive oil. Combine the remaining olive oil with the lemon juice, minced garlic, seasonings and wine, and pour over the chicken. Marinate, turning frequently, for 3 hours at room temperature or overnight in the refrigerator. Broil until golden, basting all the while with the marinade. Serve on a bed of watercress garnished with lemon slices.

*Serves 6*                                    —MRS. THOMAS H. CHOATE

⅓  cup soy sauce
juice of 1 lemon
fresh-ground pepper
legs and breasts of 2 chickens
2  handfuls fresh mint leaves

Combine the soy sauce and lemon juice and marinate the chicken (skinned, and the breasts cut in half) all day or overnight in the refrigerator, turning occasionally. When ready to bake, cover the bottom of a small casserole with mint leaves. Add a layer of chicken, fresh pepper, more mint leaves, and sprinkle with the marinade. Continue the layers until all the chicken is used. Finish with a layer of mint leaves and the remaining marinade. Cover the casserole and bake at 325° for 1½ hours or until chicken is tender. This is particularly good served with bulgur wheat. The chicken juices and marinade make a sauce.

*Serves 4*                                    —ALICE J. WISE

# MINTED CHICKEN

*Mint*
Theatrum Botanicum

# BOMBAY CHICKEN

1   chicken
flour, salt, pepper, butter
2   tbsp. brown sugar
½   cup sherry
2   tbsp. soy sauce
2   tbsp. oil
1   tbsp. minced fresh ginger
2   tbsp. sesame seeds
2   tsp. curry powder
¼   cup roughly chopped almonds
¼   cup minced celery
¼   cup minced onions

Cut the chicken into serving pieces. Dust it with salt, pepper, and flour, and brown it in butter. Place it in a baking dish, sprinkle and pour over it the next six ingredients, cover closely, and bake at 375° for 45 minutes. Remove pan from oven, uncover, and spoon off the fat. Discard all but 2 tablespoons. In a small frying pan, sauté the almonds and curry powder in the reserved fat for 3 to 4 minutes. Scrape them into the baking pan and stir to mix. Turn the chicken pieces in the sauce, sprinkle on the celery and onions, and return the pan, uncovered, to the oven. Bake 15 minutes or until chicken is lightly browned.

*Serves 4*

—MRS. C. E. ROCKWELL

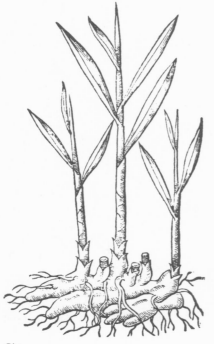

*Ginger*
The Herball

1 "oven-stuffer-roaster" chicken
1 pound chopped lamb
1 cup cooked rice or crumbs or mixture
1 medium onion, finely chopped
1 egg, lightly beaten
½ cup Marsala or any other slightly sweet wine
½ cup red wine, broth or water
1 rounded tsp. salt
fresh-ground pepper to taste

# ROASTED BONED CHICKEN STUFFED WITH LAMB

Bone the chicken, opening it down the back. Remove the thigh bones, but leave the drumstick and wing bones. (The first chicken you bone takes about an hour, but after that you can do it in 10–15 minutes.) Lay the chicken out flat, skin-side down, and use the breast fillets to cover the bare skin.

Mix the remaining ingredients and mound them in an oval from the neck to the tail of the chicken. Sew the back skin of the chicken together, overlapping it slightly and completely enclosing the stuffing. Turn it over and pat it so it looks like a slightly flattened regular chicken and tie the ends of the drumsticks neatly together.

Place the chicken in a roasting pan on a perforated rack and roast at 350°, basting with wine, broth or water about every 10 minutes. It will be beautifully browned and done in an hour and a half.

Carve this creation by cutting off the wings and legs and then slicing across. It looks very impressive on a buffet table.

*Serves 8 to 10*                           —SHAREN BENENSON

# LEMON LIME CHICKEN

2 broiling chickens, quartered
2 lemons
2 limes
salt and pepper
1 tsp. ground ginger
½ tsp. garlic powder
3 tbsp. chopped parsley
1 tbsp. chopped fresh tarragon or 1 tsp. dried
3 tbsp. snipped dill weed
sweet paprika
¼ lb. melted butter

Butter a shallow roasting pan, line with foil and butter again. Put in chicken quarters, skin side up, and sprinkle with juice of ½ lime and ½ lemon. Sprinkle herbs and seasonings over chicken in order listed. Dribble melted butter over all. Cover loosely with foil and bake 30 minutes at 375°. Remove top foil and bake 20 minutes or longer until done. **Let cool.**

Squeeze half lemon and half lime over cooked chicken. Chill. Slice remaining lemon and lime for garnish.

*Serves 4*

—MRS. LEWIS A. CLARKE

*Lemon*
De plantis epitome utilissima

70.

1  3-lb. chicken, cut up
1  tbsp. honey
1  tbsp. Worcestershire sauce
1  tsp. seasoned salt
½  tsp. ginger
¼  tsp. paprika
½  cup orange juice
¼  cup salad oil
1  cup wheat germ
1  tsp. salt

# ORANGE CRUNCH CHICKEN

In a shallow bowl mix honey, Worcestershire sauce, seasoned salt, ginger, paprika, oil and orange juice. Add chicken pieces and marinate 2 hours at room temperature or overnight in refrigerator.

Mix wheat germ and salt. Remove chicken from marinade. Coat well with wheat germ. Place coated chicken in a foil-lined pan. Bake in 350° oven 50–60 minutes or until golden brown.

*Serves 4*
—MRS. WILLIAM JENNINGS

*Sweet Beane or Carob tree*

The seede of this bean, was that kinde of weight in ancient times called karat, and amoung goldsmiths a carret, weighing sixe grains formerly, although in these dayes they account to be put foure.
—PARKINSON'S HERBAL

# CHICKEN PIE WITH CHEESE CRUST

2 small chickens
1 onion, sliced
1 carrot, sliced
1 bay leaf
salt and pepper
water
2 tbsp. butter
4 tbsp. flour
3 cups chicken broth
½ lb. mushrooms, sliced
3 hard boiled eggs, sliced
2 tbsp. chopped parsley

Place the chickens, onion, carrot, bay leaf, and salt and pepper in a stock pot, cover with water, and simmer 30 minutes or until tender. Cool chickens so they can be handled. While the chickens cook, prepare the crust below.

Remove the meat from the chicken bones and cut it into bite-size pieces. Cut the skin into coarse shreds, discarding fatty pieces. Put the chicken, skin, mushrooms, eggs, and parsley in a 10-cup casserole and mix gently. Cook the flour in the butter over low heat for 5 minutes until it is lightly browned. Add the chicken stock and stir and cook until it is thickened. Season to taste and pour into casserole. Cover the casserole with the crust, brush it with egg white, and bake at 375° for 30–35 minutes until it is lightly browned. This freezes and reheats very well.

*Serves 8*

*Apple*
The Herball

Cheese Crust
1½  cups flour
1    tsp. salt
4    tbsp. fat
3    tbsp. grated sharp cheese
3    egg yolks
2    tbsp. water

In a bowl or in a food processor, combine the salt and flour. Cut in the fat and cheese and then add the yolks and water. Wrap ball of dough and chill ½ hour before rolling out to fit casserole.

—H. B. POST

## CHICKEN IN CIDER-CREAM SAUCE

1    4-lb. chicken
5    tbsp. butter
½    cup apple cider
grated rind of 1 lemon
1    cup heavy cream
salt and pepper

Cut the chicken into serving pieces and brown in the butter. Pour the cider over the chicken, cover the pan, and simmer the chicken about 30 minutes until tender. Remove the chicken to a warm serving platter. Stir up the pan juices and scrape any brownings off the bottom. If the pan seems dry, add 2 or 3 tablespoons more cider.

Stir cream and lemon peel into the pan juices and boil to reduce slightly. Season to taste, pour the hot sauce over the chicken, and serve with rice or noodles.

*Serves 6*                    —MRS. HARDING BANCROFT

# JAMBALAYA

2 cups chopped scallions
4 large green peppers, cut in thin strips
1 cup chopped celery
3 large garlic cloves, minced
¼ lb. butter
2 sixteen-ounce cans tomatoes
1 twelve-ounce can V-8 juice
2 cups chicken broth, approximately
1 tsp. salt
½ tsp. cayenne pepper
2 cups raw rice
2 cups cooked chicken
2 cups cooked ham, cubed
2 lbs. raw shrimp, shelled

In a very large, heavy pot, sauté the scallions, pepper, celery (with some leaves), and garlic in the butter until the vegetables are soft. Add the tomatoes, juice, broth, salt and pepper and bring to a boil. Stir in the rice, return liqiud to a slow boil, cover the pot, and cook 15 minutes. Stir in the chicken and ham and if the liquid has all been absorbed, add 1 cup of broth or a glass of white wine. Cook 5 more minutes and taste rice. If it is almost done, stir in the shrimp and cook until they turn pink. The jambalaya should be a little saucy, so add more broth or a little tomato sauce if necessary, but don't overcook the rice. This is an unusual and useful party casserole.

*Serves 10*

—CHARLOTTE HENKEN

1  pt. heavy cream
1  stalk celery
5  sprigs parsley
½  tsp. Dijon mustard
1  jigger of dry sherry
pepper, salt, and nutmeg
1  envelope gelatin
½  cup rich chicken broth
2  egg yolks
1  cup thinly sliced mushrooms
1  tbsp. butter
meat of 1 cooked chicken, diced

# JELLIED CREAMED CHICKEN

In a double boiler or very heavy saucepan, place the cream, crushed celery stalk, and parsley. Reduce the liquid by half, strain, and return to pan. Add the mustard, sherry, seasonings and gelatin which has been softened in the chicken broth. Stir over low heat until the gelatine is dissolved. Beat the egg yolks, and slowly beat in some of the hot liquid. Pour the yolks into the pot and cook, stirring constantly until thickened.

Remove the pan from the heat and stir in the mushrooms, which have been sautéed in the butter, and the diced chicken. Pour into an oiled, 1-quart mold and chill several hours. Serve garnished with parsley. This is a lovely cold, summer supper dish.

*Serves 4*                    —MRS. WILLIAM C. STEERE

## CURRIED CHICKEN SALAD

2    quarts cooked, cubed chicken (about 4 chickens)
1    #2 can water chestnuts
2    lbs. seedless grapes
2    cups diced celery
2½   cups diced almonds
2    cups mayonnaise
1    tbsp. curry powder
2    tbsp. soy sauce
2    tbsp. lemon juice

Slice the water chestnuts and halve the grapes. Toss these gently with the chicken, celery, and 1½ cups of the almonds. Combine the rest of the ingredients and toss with the chicken. Chill several hours before serving. Serve on a bed of lettuce topped with the remaining almonds.
*Serves 12*       —MRS. JOHN W. SANFORD

## CHICKEN IMPERIAL

2    cups bread crumbs
¾    cup Parmesan cheese
2    cloves garlic
2    tsp. salt
½    tsp. pepper
¼    cup fresh chopped parsley
1    lb. butter
6    chicken breasts, halved, boned

Combine first six ingredients. Melt butter and soak each breast in it for 3 minutes. Roll out and press crumb mixture on each piece. Put in shallow baking dish, pour remaining butter over, and bake 45 minutes to 1 hour at 325°.
*Serves 10 to 12*       —MRS. GRAYSON L. KIRK

1   small young turkey (about 6 lbs.) cut in
    serving pieces
1   tbsp. paprika
2   large cloves garlic, crushed
salt and coarsely ground pepper to taste
1   tsp. Dijon mustard
½   cup wine vinegar
2   tbsp. lemon juice
2   bay leaves
4   tbsp. olive oil
4   tbsp. butter
½   cup chopped onions
2   cups chicken broth
2   green peppers, seeded and sliced
¼   cup canned pimientos, sliced
12  large pitted olives, sliced

# TURKEY CASSEROLE

Place the turkey pieces in a bowl. Blend paprika, garlic, salt and pepper, mustard and lemon juice and rub this mixture into the turkey pieces. Add vinegar and bay leaves, mix again and let stand for two or three hours. Then drain the turkey, sauté in combined oil and butter until golden brown on all sides, add onions, stir and sauté 2 or 3 minutes longer. Add chicken broth, cover and cook slowly for about 2 hours or until meat is tender. Add all other ingredients and simmer 15 more minutes.

*Serves 6*
                              —MARY AMBROSE

# BRAISED YOUNG TURKEY

1   young turkey (5 lbs.)
salt and pepper
4   tbsp. lard
3   carrots, minced
1   small turnip, minced
2   stalks celery, minced
2   onions, minced
1   clove garlic, minced
thin sheets of fresh pork fat
bouquet garni (bay leaf, thyme, tarragon)
2   tomatoes, quartered
3   cups chicken broth
3   tbsp. beurre manié

Wipe the turkey inside and out with a damp cloth, season inside and out with salt and pepper. Heat the lard in a casserole and brown the turkey on all sides. Remove and keep warm. Put the carrots, celery, turnip and onions in the casserole, add a little more lard if necessary and cook until the vegetables are soft and golden. Season with salt and pepper, add garlic and mix well. Remove the vegetables from the casserole with a slotted spoon.

Line the bottom and sides of the casserole with the sheets of pork fat and put turkey in the casserole. Add the vegetables, bouquet garni, the tomatoes and the broth. Cover the turkey with another sheet of pork fat.

Cover the casserole, bring the liquid to a boil and then put the casserole in a preheated 350° oven for about 1¾ hours. Remove the turkey, put it on a serving dish and keep hot. Skim the fat off the liquid in the casserole, strain through a fine sieve, let stand for 5 minutes and skim fat off again. Return sauce to low heat, stir in beurre manié. You should use 1 tablespoon of beurre manié for each cup of braising liquid. Simmer for 10 minutes, correct seasoning and serve the sauce separately in a sauceboat. Garnish platter on which turkey is served with watercress.

*Serves 6* —NANCY HECKSHIRE

1  *small (6–8 lbs.) turkey*
1  *cup white wine*
1  *cup olive oil*
¼  *cup minced tarragon*
*salt and pepper*

Have the turkey split in half and the backbone removed. Sprinkle the halves with salt, pepper, and tarragon and put them in a heavy plastic bag. Add the wine and oil, close the bag, and soak the turkey overnight. Rotate the bag from time to time to mix.

Broil the turkey over hot coals for 1 hour or more until the juices which run from the pierced thigh are no longer pink. Baste often with the marinade. This makes a nice change for cooking out.

*Serves 8* —MRS. LANGDON S. SIMONS

# BABY TURKEY TARRAGON

*Grape*
Kreuterbuch (Lonitzer)

# SALMI OF DUCK

1 duck (5 lbs.)

8 tbsp. lard

salt and pepper to taste

¼ cup Armagnac brandy

¼ cup minced fat from Virginia or prosciutto ham

20 very small white onions, 4 of them stuck with 2 cloves each

6 shallots, minced

4 tbsp. flour

¼ lb. salt pork, blanched and finely diced

1 bouquet garni

pinch of nutmeg

4 cups dry red wine

8 slices of French bread

6 tbsp. butter or lard

1 clove of garlic

Cut the duck in serving pieces. Heat the lard in a large, heavy casserole until it is very hot, and brown the duck pieces on all sides. Pour all fat off casserole, season the duck pieces with salt and pepper, sprinkle them with Armagnac, and flame.

Remove the duck pieces and the pan juices from casserole and reserve. Add the ham fat to the casserole and sauté until the fat is rendered. Then add the shallots and white onions and cook over gentle heat until the onions are golden brown. Sprinkle with flour and stir well, then add the diced salt pork, nutmeg and the bouquet garni. Stir in the wine and bring to a boil. Add the duck pieces and their pan juice, correct seasoning, and simmer over low heat for an hour or until duck is tender. Fry the bread slices in butter or lard until

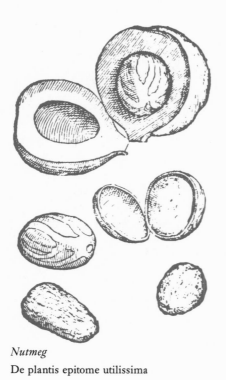

*Nutmeg*
De plantis epitome utilissima

golden, then rub on both sides with the garlic clove. Remove duck to hot serving platter, strain the sauce through a fine sieve, reduce quickly by about 1/3 of the volume, then pour over duck. Garnish the dish with the fried bread slices.
*Serves 4*
—ROBERTO DᴇVIRA

# DANISH STYLE WILD DUCK

1    *wild duck*
*flour, salt and pepper to dredge*
2–3  *tbsp. butter*
2    *cups heavy cream*
¼    *cup scallions, minced*
*salt and pepper to taste*

Dredge wild duck in seasoned flour, then brown in butter. Put the duck in a heavy pan with a cover. Bring the cream to a simmer and pour over the duck. Cover the pot and let it simmer slowly on the back of the stove for an hour, turning the duck once. Remove the cover, stir in the scallions, and continue simmering 20–30 minutes as sauce thickens. Remove duck to warm platter, season sauce to taste, and serve unstrained. One teaspoon pink or green peppercorns may be added to the sauce in the last 10 minutes of cooking instead of the traditional fresh-ground black pepper at the end.
*Serves 2 to 3*
—MRS. HENRY E. COE III

# ROAST
# PHEASANTS
# OR
# PARTRIDGES

This is my mother, Lady Cockburn-Fairburn's method with game birds. Allow a brace of pheasants for 6 to 8 diners or 1 partridge for 2 diners. Wipe the insides of the birds with a muslin cloth rinsed in lemon juice. Place inside each bird:

3   *nut-size pieces of sweet butter rolled in*
    *minced onion*
    *minced parsley*
    *minced thyme.*

Place 2 pieces unsmoked bacon on each breast, cover with foil, and roast at 350° for about 45 minutes. When birds are tender, remove them from the oven, discard the foil and bacon, dredge the breasts with flour, and add a glass of red wine to the pan juices. Return the birds to the oven and allow the breasts to "froth." These are a great favorite served at room temperature for a cold buffet supper.

If you wish to serve the birds hot, make a sauce as follows:

Simmer the giblets in beef broth with a fresh bouquet garni while the birds roast. Run the excess fat off the roasting pan juices and add the juices to the giblet broth. Add 6 ounces of finely chopped black olives and a teaspoon of tomato puree and simmer to reduce the juices by half. Serve with the carved birds.

—MRS. FREDERICK P. HOUSTON

## PHEASANT IN SOUR CREAM SAUCE

1   pheasant
flour, butter, oil
½   bay leaf
1   sprig basil (½ tsp. dried)
1   sprig rosemary (½ tsp. dried)
salt and pepper
½   cup white wine
1   cup sliced fresh mushrooms
½   cup sour cream

Cut each pheasant into serving pieces, dust with flour, and brown in a mixture of butter and oil. Add herbs, salt and pepper, and pour over the wine. Cover tightly and simmer slowly on top of stove or bake at 325° for 1 hour or more until the meat is very tender. Remove the pheasant pieces to a warm serving platter. Place the pan over high heat and cook the mushrooms 3 or 4 minutes while stirring and scraping up any brown bits. Remove the pan from the heat, quickly stir in the sour cream, and pour the sauce over the pheasant. Serve with wild rice.

*Serves 2 to 4*                          —MRS. PETER GARVAN

## SAM'S GAME BIRD NO-FAIL METHOD

Preheat oven to 450°. Rub bird inside and out with butter, salt and pepper. Place bird on a rack in a roasting pan with a tight-fitting cover. Add water or ½ water, ½ wine, to pan till it reaches the bottom of the rack. Cover tightly. Put strips of aluminum foil between the lid and pan to improve seal if necessary. Roast 15–20 minutes per pound. Duck, pheasant, goose, and wild turkey all respond well to this method and do not dry out. The tight-fitting lid and very hot oven are the secret.

—MRS. HENRY E. COE III

# Meat

# STEAK WITH BROCCOLI
(Cantonese Style)

1 lb. skirt steak
1 large head broccoli
1 slice fresh ginger (size of a quarter)
¼ cup water mixed with ¼ cup of oyster sauce + 2 tbsp. cornstarch
dash of pepper
3 tbsp. vegetable oil
1 tsp. sugar
¾ to 1 cup chicken broth or water
1 small clove of garlic

Marinade for Beef:

3 tsp. cornstarch
3 tsp. soy sauce (light)
2 tsp. sherry (optional)
1 tsp. salt
1 tsp. oil
1 tsp. sugar

Slice steak against grain into 1-inch × ½-inch pieces and marinate while preparing broccoli. Wash broccoli and peel off tough outer layer. Slice stems diagonally and separate florets into 3 or 4 sections.

Crush garlic and place garlic and ginger in heated oil. Remove steak from marinade and stir fry to rare or medium rare. Remove from pan and set aside.

Add a little oil to wok if necessary and heat, add salt and the drained broccoli. Stir fry and add water or broth. Cover and cook to desired tenderness; add steak, stir a bit and add oyster sauce mixture and sugar; stir and heat to boiling, and remove immediately. Serve over white rice.

*Serves 4*                                    —INA LEONG

1½    lb. flank steak

Marinade:

½    cup thin soy sauce
3    tbsp. honey
2    tbsp. vinegar
1    garlic clove, minced
1    tsp. powdered ginger
¾    cup salad oil
5    stalks scallions, chopped

# MARINATED FLANK STEAK

Mix the marinade and add the steak. Marinate overnight, turning occasionally. Broil steak to taste, indoors or outdoors, brushing with marinade. This marinade is also very good with lamb chops.

*Serves 2 to 3*

—DAVID PACE

# SALT BROILED STEAK

Build a wood fire on a flat stone. When the stone is white with heat remove the wood entirely. Then take a steak, cover both sides thickly with salt. Place the steak on the stone. Turn from side to side. Result most delicious.

—MRS. ALBERT P. LOENING

## MY FAVORITE HAMBURGER

1 lb. well ground sirloin steak
salt and pepper to taste
2 tsp. club soda

Mix all ingredients. The patties puff up and are juicy if cooked 3 minutes on each side under a hot broiler.

*Serves 4*

—ENID A. HAUPT

## MEATBALLS ESPANOL

1 lb. lean ground beef
1 cup soft bread crumbs
1–4 each finely chopped onion and celery
1½ tsp. Worcestershire sauce
1 egg
2 cloves garlic, crushed
pepper to taste
1 can (16 oz.) stewed tomatoes
2½ cups zucchini thinly sliced
½ tsp. each, crushed oregano, basil, sugar
1 tbsp. cornstarch
1 cup beef broth
3 cups cooked rice

Combine beef, bread crumbs, onion, celery, egg, Worcestershire sauce, garlic, salt and pepper. Mix thoroughly. Form into 12 meatballs. Place in greased shallow baking pan. Bake at 375° for 20 minutes. Meanwhile, combine tomatoes, zucchini and seasonings and simmer 5 minutes. Blend cornstarch and broth. Stir into tomato mixture. Pour over meatballs. Continue baking 10 minutes longer. Serve with cooked rice.

*Serves 6*

—SYLVIA STEIN

1 pound lean ground beef
½ cup finely chopped onions
½ cup soft bread crumbs
¾ tsp. salt
¼ tsp. ground black pepper
2 tbsp. vegetable oil
3 oz. cream cheese, softened
⅓ cup grated Parmesan cheese
¼ cup snipped fresh parsley
1 tbsp. fresh basil leaves
1 clove garlic, minced
1 cup hot beef broth
1 tsp. cornstarch
2 cups hot cooked rice

# MEATBALLS WITH SAUCE VERTE

Combine meat, onions, bread crumbs, ½ teaspoon salt, and pepper; mix thoroughly. Form into 8 balls 1½ inches in diameter. Brown on all sides in oil. Drain off fat. Combine remaining ingredients except cornstarch and rice; blend until smooth. Pour over meatballs, cover and simmer 15 minutes. Stir 2 tablespoons water into cornstarch. Pour into sauce; cook, stirring constantly, about 1 minute or until thickened. Serve over beds of fluffy rice.

*Serves 4*

—ROBERTO DeVIRA

*Basil*
Theatrum Botanicum

# MOLDAVIAN STUFFED CABBAGE

2 pounds ground beef
1 cup rice
1 large onion
1 large cabbage
1 32-oz. pkg. sauerkraut
½ cup bread crumbs (plain)
1 8-oz. can tomato sauce
1 small bunch of fresh dill
1 small bunch of fresh parsley leaves
2 cups chicken broth
ground black pepper, paprika, salt to taste
1 tbsp. wheat germ
½ cup corn oil

*Cabbage*
De plantis epitome utilissima

### The stuffing

Simmer the finely chopped onion with ½ cup of corn oil adding from time to time 2–3 tablespoons of water, till becomes very soft; add the rice and stir continually for about 5 minutes; take it off the stove and add ground pepper, paprika, ½ cup chicken broth, wheat germ, salt and the finely chopped dill and parsley leaves and the ground beef and mix everything very well.

### The cabbage leaves

Bring water to boiling (1 gallon water) in a large and deep pot and add 1 tablespoon of salt; cut the cabbage around the core but do not remove its core. Dump the whole cabbage in the boiling water and cook it for about 3–4 minutes one side and 3–4 minutes the other side, then with a large fork unwrap each leaf and take them out of the pot. Deepen the cut around the core and repeat the operation till all leaves of 5 inch length have been removed. When the leaves are cool enough for handling, take them one by one and cut out the ribs. Fold each leaf over 1 tablespoon of the stuffing and roll it up.

At the bottom of a large clay or glass pot, put half of the sauerkraut, then fill in with the stuffed cabbage rolls and on top of them the rest of the sauerkraut, the rest of the chicken broth, and the tomato sauce as a top dressing. Put the pot in the oven at 350° and cook it for about 2 hours, then turn the heat down to 200° and keep the pot in the oven for another hour, after which it's ready to be served.

*Serves 8 to 10*                          —FLORITZA DIACONESCU

# PICADILLO À LA CUBANA

1   *lb. top round ground*
1   *can tomato paste*
½   *bottle olives (chopped)*
1   *handful raisins*
1   *yellow onion (chopped)*
1   *green pepper (chopped)*
½   *can pimientos (chopped)*
¼   *cup sherry*
1   *lemon (juice of)*
3   *tbsp. butter*
*salt and pepper to taste*

Mix ingredients in a bowl. Allow to stand 15 minutes (or more). Cook slowly in 3 tablespoons butter in heavy skillet for 20 minutes. Serve on platter topped with 4 fried eggs and surrounded with fried bananas and fluffy rice.

*Serves 4*                          —MRS. JULIO G. HERRERA

# HUNGARIAN RAGOUT

3 lbs. stew beef, cut in 1-inch cubes
¼ cup butter
¼ cup oil
4 tbsp. Hungarian sweet paprika
1 tbsp. tomato paste
2 large onions, chopped
1 cup red wine (or enough to cover meat)
1½ cups sour cream
2 tbsp. dried dill weed
salt and pepper to taste

In a kettle, heat butter and oil, blend in paprika and tomato paste. Add beef, stir and cook until coated with paprika and well browned. Stir in onions and cook for 2 minutes. Pour in wine, cover kettle and simmer for 2 hours, until beef is tender. Just before serving, stir in sour cream and seasonings; reheat but do not allow to boil. Serve on noodles or rice.

*Serves 6* —EILEEN K. SCHOFIELD

1½   cups cold pot roast, or roast beef (chopped)
1½   cups cold boiled potatoes (chopped)
1½   cups boiled beets (chopped)
1    small onion (optional)
⅓    cup of beef fat (optional)
3    tbsp. butter
beef gravy
salt and pepper to taste

# RED FLANNEL HASH

Mix beef, potatoes, and beets. Season to taste, using onion if desired, and mix in beef fat.

Melt butter in cast-iron skillet. Add hash. Turn flame low and allow to cook ½ hour to 1 hour. Add rich beef gravy and beet juice in equal parts from time to time. It will take up a considerable amount while cooking. Should be a moist but not too liquid consistency. Just before serving, allow to brown thoroughly. Turn onto platter. Dot with butter. Serve with cole slaw.

*Serves 4*                              —MRS. W. J. ROBBINS

*Parsley*

*The leaves of parsley eaten after onoins, leeks of garlicke, taketh away the offensive smell of them; they use also to cast the herbe into their fish ponds if there be any sicke fish among them to cleanse them.*
                              —PARKINSON'S HERBAL

# BEEF ROLL-UPS

8    slices beef bracciole
3    tbsp. butter
3    tbsp. salad oil
1    clove minced garlic
½    cup minced mushrooms
½    cup minced onions
1    cup crumbled Pepperidge Farm dressing
1–2  tbsp. minced parsley
salt and pepper to taste
1    can consommé
1    cup red wine
brandy to deglaze pan
flour to coat meat
1    cup sour cream

Sauté garlic in 2 tablespoons butter and 1 tablespoon oil for 1 minute. Add onions and mushrooms and continue to sauté without browning until soft. Add stuffing, parsley, salt and pepper, and mix well. Place a generous tablespoon of mixture on the wide end of each piece of pounded meat. Tuck in ends and roll up. Fasten with a round toothpick.

Dust each roll with flour, shaking off excess. Brown in remaining butter and oil and remove to covered casserole. Deglaze pan with brandy and pour over rolls. Add consommé and red wine. Bake at 350° 1½ hours, turning occasionally. If too much liquid accumulates, remove lid to allow some to evaporate. Otherwise, leave casserole covered. Five minutes before serving, stir ¼ cup hot liquid into sour cream and then return all to liquid in casserole and stir gently.

Correct seasoning, cover and heat through. Serve with rice.

*Note*: An Italian flavor can be achieved by adding 1 tablespoon oregano and 1 tablespoon pine nuts to stuffing and by substituting spaghetti sauce for the sour cream.

*Serves 4*                    —MRS. JAMES W. RILEY, JR.

# BEEF STEW

| | |
|---|---|
| 2 | *lbs. top sirloin, cut in cubes* |
| ¼ | *lb. sweet butter* |
| 2 | *tbsp. flour* |
| 5–6 | *cups good, rich beef broth* |
| 1 | *tsp. dried parsley* |
| 1 | *bay leaf* |
| ½ | *tsp. dried thyme* |
| ¼ | *tsp. black pepper* |
| 8 | *small carrots, skinned and cut up* |
| 4 | *or more ribs celery, skinned and cut up* |
| 18 | *small white onions, peeled* |
| 2 | *tbsp. butter plus two tbsp. flour, mixed, (beurre manié) to thicken sauce at end of recipe* |

Sauté meat in butter until just brown all over. Transfer to heated casserole. Add flour and stir to blend. Add heated broth and seasonings. Bring to boil, then simmer for an hour. Add vegetables and simmer for another hour. When done, thicken sauce with beurre manié to desired thickness.

*Serves 6 to 8*              —MRS. JOHN E. PARSONS

# CURRIED SOUR CREAM STEW

½ lb. mushrooms
1½ tsp. butter or margarine
2 lbs. stewing beef, cut into cubes
2 large onions, sliced
1 tbsp. curry powder
1 cup consommé
1 cup dry red wine
1½ tbsp. flour
1 tbsp. horseradish
2 cups sour cream
2 cups green frozen peas partly cooked

Sauté mushrooms in butter. Add beef, onions, curry powder, consommé and red wine. Bring to a boil. Cover. Bake at 325° for 1½ hours or until beef is tender. Combine flour with small amount of water to make a smooth paste. Stir into hot mixture. Add horseradish and sour cream and salt. Reheat if necessary but do not boil. Add peas. Serve over hot cooked rice.

To prepare ahead: Follow directions to and including the thickening. Reheat and then add horseradish and sour cream and peas.

*Serves 4* —MRS. WILLIAM F. YOUNG

*Pea*
Kreuterbuch (Lonitzer)

3 lbs. pork loin
1 quart beer
1 tbsp. salt
fresh-ground pepper
2 cloves
1 bay leaf
½ tsp. thyme
6 stems parsley
¼ cup sugar (approximately)
currant jelly

# COLD PORK LOIN ARGENTINE

Place the pork loin in a casserole that approximates it in size and shape. Pour in the beer and add all the other ingredients except the sugar and jelly. Cover and bring to a boil on top of the stove. Cook in a 250° oven for 2½ hours. Cool loin in the broth. Cover the cooled loin with sugar and run under a broiler to brown. Slice thin and serve with currant jelly on the side.

*Serves 6 to 8*                    —JANET R. HESTER

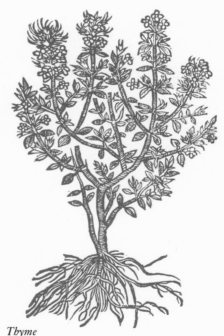

*Thyme*
Theatrum Botanicum

*Thyme*

Taken with hoy, licoris and aniseed in wine, it helpeth a dry cough, and is comfortable broth for the head. The distilled water thereof appyed with vinegar of Roses to the forehead, eseth the rage of Frenye, and expelleth vertigo that is the swimming or the turning of the braine.

—PARKINSON'S HERBAL

# PORK CHOPS WITH GIN AND ORANGE JUICE

6 pork chops
flour
salt and pepper to taste
1 clove garlic, minced
rind of one orange, grated
juice of the orange ( ½ cup)
½ cup gin
chopped parsley

Salt and pepper chops and brown in one layer. Sprinkle on garlic and orange rind, then combine orange juice and gin and pour over top. Cover and cook slowly over low heat for 45 minutes or until tender. Serve sprinkled with parsley, with rice on the side.

*Serves 4*                    —MRS. HAROLD G. BARKER

# BAKED PORK CHOPS WITH MINT

4 large, lean pork chops
1 tsp. grated lemon rind
1 tsp. grated orange rind
pinch each salt, pepper, nutmeg
1 tbsp. minced parsley
¼ cup shredded mint
juice of ½ lemon and ½ orange
1 tbsp. sugar

Place the chops in one layer in a casserole with a tight-fitting cover. Sprinkle over them the rind, seasonings, and herbs. Heat and stir the juices and sugar until the sugar dissolves and pour over the meat. Bake, covered, at 350° for 2 hours.

*Serves 4*                    —IRENE BALLENGER

10 pork chops, ¾" thick
salt and pepper to taste
flour for dredging
oil to brown chops
2 tbsp. butter
2 tbsp. shallots, chopped
10 oz. mushrooms, sliced
2 tbsp. cognac
2 tbsp. Dijon mustard
¾ cup heavy cream
parsley or watercress, minced

# PORK CHOPS IN MUSTARD SAUCE

Season chops and brown well, a few at a time, in a heavy skillet. Remove to a plate and pour fat from pan. Return the pan to the heat, melt the butter, and stir in the shallots and mushrooms. Cover and cook over low heat for five minutes. Return chops to pan, sprinkle on cognac and ignite it. While it flames, stir the cream into the mustard, and when the flames die, add to the pan. Cover and simmer 20 to 30 minutes until chops are cooked and tender.

Remove chops to a heated platter. Stir sauce, scraping bottom of pan. Stir in more butter, in bits, or cognac, if desired. Pour over chops and garnish with parsley, or even better, chopped watercress. Serve with rice.

*Serves 6* —MARY HOMANS

*Mustard*
Theatrum Botanicum

# PORK PIE

Pastry:

1  heaping cup sifted flour
6  tbsp. shortening or lard
½  tsp. salt
1  tsp. summer savory or marjoram
2  tbsp. ice water

Thoroughly combine first four ingredients in a food processor using the cutting blade. Then, slowly add ice water. Wrap ball of dough in waxed paper and chill at least one hour. (You can also make this crust by the conventional method.) Roll out crust and fit in a 9″ pie plate.

Filling:

1  lb. ground pork
1  small onion, finely chopped
1  clove garlic, finely chopped
½  tsp. savory or marjoram
¼  tsp. ground cloves
¼  tsp. celery seed
salt and pepper
½  cup cream
1  egg
one large, soft, cooking apple, quartered and sliced thinly

Cook meat and seasonings in a skillet until the liquid evaporates. Spoon it into the pie shell and pour over it the egg and cream beaten together. Bake 20 minutes at 350°. Arrange apple slices over top and bake 20 to 25 minutes more until apples are lightly browned and soft.

Serves 6                                    —SHAREN BENENSON

*Marjoram*
The Herball

½ lb. bulk pork sausage

1 cup chopped onions

½ cup chopped green pepper

1 large eggplant, peeled and cubed (about 1 pound)

1 can (15 ounces) tomato sauce

1 tbsp. each fresh basil and oregano leaves

1 tsp. salt

1 clove garlic, minced

¼ tsp. ground black pepper

3 cups cooked rice

½ lb. mozzarella cheese, grated (2 cups)

# SAUSAGE AND EGGPLANT SKILLET

In a large skillet crumble sausage and cook until well done. Drain off excess fat. Add onions, green pepper, and eggplant. Cook about 5 minutes. Stir in tomato sauce and seasonings. Cover and simmer 10 minutes or until eggplant is translucent. Add rice and 1 cup cheese. Heat thoroughly. Sprinkle remaining cheese on top and allow to melt.

*Serves 6 to 8*

—ALIDA HAYES

# GARBANZOS CON CHORIZOS
## (Chick Peas and Sausage)

3 cans chick peas
6 chorizos or 6 Italian hot sausage
1 16-oz. can tomatoes with tomato paste and basil
4 onions
2 tbsp. olive oil
1 tbsp. sugar
1 clove garlic, crushed
salt, pepper and a few dashes of Tabasco

Cook and brown sausage. Set aside. Thinly slice the onions and fry in olive oil until golden. Add the can of tomatoes. Simmer together, uncovered, for about 20 to 30 minutes to make a sauce. In the meantime, drain the liquid from 3 or 4 cans of chick peas and put them in a buttered casserole. Season the tomato sauce with salt, pepper, Tabasco, sugar and garlic powder and pour over the chick peas. Cut up the sausage into small chunks and add. Gently mix all together. Bake, covered, in 350° oven for 45 minutes.

This can be served as an entree or a side dish. Serves 8 to 10 as an entree or 20 as an accompaniment. I often serve it for patio parties with barbecued meat and a salad. It can be made ahead, and a delay in serving dinner will only enhance the flavor. Just turn the oven low, cover and let it sit.

*Serves 8 to 10*                    —DOROTHY GREENLEE

1   lb. ground pork
1   egg
salt and pepper
½   cup soft bread crumbs
2   tbsp. milk
¼   cup parsley, chopped
½   cup red onion, chopped
butter
3   cups chicken broth
½   cup white wine
1   tbsp. cornstarch
½   cup yogurt
¼   cup capers, chopped
3   anchovy fillets, chopped

# GERMAN KLOPSE

Mix pork, egg, and salt and pepper. Add bread crumbs moistened with milk. Wilt onion in butter and mix it and parsley into meat mixture. Mold meat mixture into 1″ balls.

Stir wine into cornstarch and add to broth in a wide bottom sauce pan or enameled skillet. Cook until slightly thickened. Add "Klopse" to simmering broth. Stir gently until broth returns to simmer. Then cover and cook gently about 15 minutes. Break one "Klopse" open to be sure they are done. Remove from heat and stir in yogurt, capers and anchovies. Serve with rice.

*Serves 4*                    —MRS. CURTIS LANGER

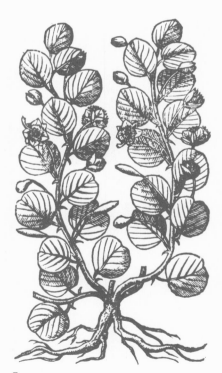

*Caper*
The Herball

## PORK BALLS FOR ANY CLEAR SOUP

½ lb. lean raw pork
6 tbsp. bread crumbs
1 egg
2 tbsp. heavy cream
1 tbsp. onion
1 tsp. caraway seed
1 tbsp. parsley
salt and pepper

Grind all ingredients together until homogenous. Form into about 20 little balls. Poach about 5 minutes in any clear broth, one cup per person. These make a meal for two people or an elegant first course for 6. Sprinkle a little parsley or watercress, chopped fine, on top.

*Serves 2*
—SHAREN BENENSON

## BRAISED LAMB SHANKS

2 tbsp. butter
2 lamb shanks
½ cup onions, sliced
½ cup chicken bouillon
½ tsp. dried rosemary
garlic to taste
salt and pepper

Brown the lamb shanks in butter together with the onion in a Dutch oven or other oven-proof casserole. Add the broth, garlic and rosemary. Cover and place on a small burner and simmer for about two hours until the meat is very tender and the liquid is reduced and browning.

*Serves 2*
—MRS. C. VICTOR WILLIAMS

1   small leg of lamb, boned and flattened out
1   onion, chopped
¼   cup chopped parsley
1   stalk celery, chopped
1   tsp. rosemary
2   tbsp. butter
2   cup cooked wild rice
salt to taste
½   cup dry red wine
½   cup beef consommé (homemade or canned)
¼   cup currant jelly

# ROLLED LAMB WITH WILD RICE STUFFING

Sauté onion and celery in butter. Mix rice, parsley, rosemary and salt. Add to onion and celery. Mix. Place stuffing in center of flattened lamb; roll, and tie securely. Sprinkle with salt and pepper. Roast at 325°, fifteen minutes per pound.

After first fifteen or twenty minutes of roasting, baste with following: Mix wine, consommé and jelly in saucepan and heat. Use to baste lamb. Baste frequently. Skim off fat; use drippings and bastings as sauce for meat when served.

*Serves 6*
—LIZA FOSBURGH

*Sage*
Theatrum Botanicum

*Sage*

*Sage is of excellent good use to helpe the memory, by warming and quickening the senses.*
—PARKINSON'S HERBAL

# TIPSY LAMB

1 8–10 lb. leg of lamb, boned and butterflied

Marinade

3   carrots, chopped
2   yellow onions, chopped
1   tsp. whole peppercorns
6   sprigs parsley
3   sprigs fresh, or ½ tsp. dried thyme
2   bay leaves
¾   cup red wine vinegar
1   bottle red wine
¼   cup olive oil
¼   cup gin
1   tbsp. salt

Sauce

marinade
2 tbsp. flour
2 tbsp. butter
2 tbsp. fresh or 1 ½ tsp. dried tarragon
salt and pepper

Combine marinade ingredients and let stand in a closed glass container, covered and unrefrigerated, overnight. Next day lay lamb in a glass dish, pour marinade over it and refrigerate, turning once or twice a day, for 5 days. When ready to cook, remove lamb from marinade and pat it dry. Grill it over charcoal about 20 minutes each side so that it is still pink inside.

While grilling the lamb, pour the marinade in a saucepan and boil it to reduce it by half. Strain the marinade and return it to the pan. Make a roux of the butter and flour and add it in bits to the simmering marinade, stirring constantly.

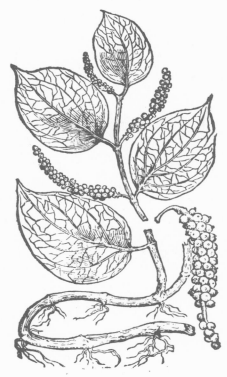

*Pepper*
The Herball

When sauce reaches desired thickness, stir in tarragon and simmer 10 minutes. Correct seasoning and pass hot sauce with sliced lamb.
*Serves 10*                                                    —MARY HOMANS


| | |
|---|---|
| 6 | small lamb shanks |
| 1 | cup dry vermouth |
| 1 | cup salad oil |
| 3 | shallots or one med. onion, minced |
| 2 | cloves garlic, minced |
| 1 | tbsp. lemon juice |
| 1 | tsp. salt |
| 1 | tsp. tarragon, finely chopped |
| 1 | tsp. basil, finely chopped |
| 10 | peppercorns, crushed |

# MARINATED LAMB SHANKS

Place shanks in a shallow pan in one layer. Mix the rest of the ingredients well and pour over the shanks. Cover and refrigerate 24 hours, turning the shanks several times. Broil the shanks, six inches from the flame, 30 minutes. Turn them frequently and baste liberally with the marinade. These are delicious cooked on an outdoor grill.
*Serves 6*                                              —MRS. HENRY STANLEY

# GRILLED, MARINATED LEG OF LAMB

1  6-lb. leg of lamb, boned and butterflied

Marinade:

salt and pepper to taste
1    cup chopped, fresh mint
¼   cup lemon juice
½   cup dry vermouth
½   cup olive oil
1    onion, sliced in thin rings

Rub lamb with salt and pepper. Place in a glass or enameled dish. Mix marinade, and pour it over lamb. Cover and refrigerate 24 hours, turning occasionally. Cook lamb over charcoal fire or in broiler, turning, and basting frequently with marinade.

Serve sliced, garnished with more fresh mint, chopped finely. If any marinade is left over, put it through the blender, heat to boiling, stir in butter and lemon juice to taste, and pass with the lamb.

*Serves 6*                          —MARY HOMANS

Commentarii

7   lb. boned, rolled leg of lamb
2   garlic cloves, cut in slivers
salad oil
salt and pepper
1   tsp. rosemary
½   tsp. thyme
¼   cup Pernod

**A**ge the lamb in your own refrigerator three or four days. When ready to cook, make small holes in the lamb with a pointed paring knife and insert the garlic slivers. Rub all over with oil, then with salt and pepper and then with the herbs. Insert a meat thermometer and roast to the "medium rare beef" reading. It takes about two hours. Remove from oven and "rest" fifteen minutes. Keep warm until serving if you can't serve it immediately. Just before serving, flame it using ¼ cup of Pernod.

Sauce Tomate au Pastis

1   tbsp. olive oil
¾   cup onion, chopped
2   cups tomato sauce
½   tsp. crushed bay leaf
½   tsp. thyme
1   tsp. sugar
¼   cup Pernod
salt and pepper
pan drippings from lamb

Wilt the onion in the oil. Add the rest of the ingredients to the pan and simmer 20 minutes.

*Serves 8 to 10*                    —SHAREN BENENSON

# STUFFED CABBAGE

1   medium head of cabbage
1   lb. of chopped lamb
2   cans tomato sauce
1½  cups cooked rice
1   large onion finely chopped
1   large can of sauerkraut
1   clove garlic, crushed
salt and pepper to taste
1   egg

Remove outer leaves of cabbage. Place cabbage into a large pot, cover with water, bring to a boil. Simmer until soft. Remove and core, carefully remove leaves.

Mix beef, rice, onion, garlic, egg, salt, and pepper. Place on cabbage leaves, fold both sides and roll, secure with wooden toothpick. Mix sauerkraut and tomato sauce. Place layer on bottom of large pot (with cover). Place layer of cabbage rolls and then layer of sauerkraut, ending with cabbage rolls. Cover and cook for one hour at simmer. This recipe can be used as a main dish or rolled smaller as an appetizer.

*Serves 6*
—JOAN BOWE

*Cabbage*
Kreuterbuch (Lonitzer)

2 pounds ground lamb
2 onions, chopped
1 whole nutmeg, grated
4 tomatoes, peeled, chopped coarsely, salted and
  peppered
½ tsp. oregano
½ tsp. thyme
½ tsp. sugar
8 small zucchinis
2 small eggplants
½ pound fresh grated Parmesan cheese
6 tbsp. butter
6 tbsp. flour
1 tsp. cinnamon
3 cups milk (or Half and Half)

# MOUSSAKA

Brown meat in large saucepan until crumbly. Add onion, nutmeg, cinnamon, herbs, salt, pepper, tomatoes. Cook 20 minutes. Set aside. Trim ends off zucchini, slice and peel. Dice eggplant. Steam zucchini and eggplant (or sauté) for a few minutes. Season. Spread in a flat baking dish about 9″ × 14″. Sprinkle with ⅓ cheese. Spread meat mixture on top and another ⅓ cheese.

Make sauce with butter, flour and milk. Season with salt. Spoon over surface and sprinkle with rest of cheese. Bake in 375° oven for 1 hour. Let stand 5 minutes. Carve in squares.

Can be made day before except for sauce.

*Serves 10*
                    —MRS. F. DAVID LAPHAM

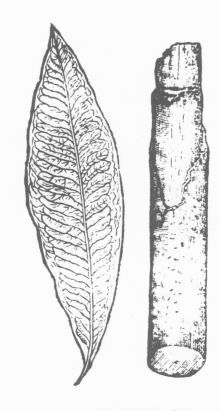

*Cinnamon*
The Herball

# VEAL AND WATER CHESTNUTS

¼    lb. butter
2½   lbs. veal cut in 1½ inch cubes
1    onion, finely chopped
1    clove garlic, minced
½    cup celery, chopped
1    tsp. salt, ½ tsp. pepper
1    lb. fresh mushrooms, sliced
1    cup beef broth
8-oz. sliced water chestnuts
2    cups heavy cream
¼    cup brandy
2    bay leaves
¼    cup chopped parsley

Melt ½ of the butter in an ovenproof casserole and sauté the veal lightly until gray. Remove the veal and sauté the onion, garlic, salt and pepper. Return the veal to the casserole and remove from heat. Melt the remaining butter in a skillet and sauté the mushrooms and celery. Add the mushrooms, celery, beef broth, water chestnuts and bay leaves to veal. Place in oven (375° preheated) and cook covered 1½ hours. (All this can be done ahead of time and refrigerated. When ready to use, add the cream and simmer on top of stove for 15 to 20 minutes. Just before serving, add the brandy and parsley.

*Serves 6 to 8*                    —MRS. WILLIAM F. YOUNG

4 lbs. veal, cubed
½ cup flour
1 tsp. salt
½ tsp. pepper
½ cup butter
½ cup diced onion
½ lb. sliced mushrooms
3 springs rosemary (1 tsp. crushed, dried)
¼ cup chopped parsley
1 cup dry white wine
2 tbsp. lemon juice
1 tsp. sugar
2 cups stewed tomatoes

# HERBED VEAL

Place the flour, salt, and pepper in a bag and mix. Add the veal and shake to coat all the pieces. Melt the butter in a large skillet and brown the veal. It's better to brown several batches than to crowd the pan. Reserve the browned veal and sauté the onions and mushrooms in the same pan. Sprinkle on the flour left in the bag while they are cooking. Add the rosemary and parsley and pour in the wine. Raise the heat and stir and scrape until the bottom is clean and you have a thick, smooth sauce. Stir in the lemon juice and tomatoes. Add the veal, bring to a simmer, and cook 45 minutes, covered. Serve with rice.

*Serves 8 to 10*                    —ELEANOR ISDALE

*Rosemary*
The Herball

113.

# MARIE'S VEAL BIRDS HOLSTEIN

8 slices veal scallopine

Stuffing:

2 hard boiled eggs, quartered
¼ cup chopped onion
¼ cup chopped mushrooms
¼ cup chopped celery
1 cup soft bread crumbs
salt and pepper to taste
1 pinch each parsley, tarragon, dill, and marjoram
garlic if desired
3 tbsp. butter
3 tbsp. oil
flour to dredge veal
1 can consommé
white wine or sherry
brandy to deglaze pan
3 tbsp. heavy cream
1 cup sour cream

Sauté onions, mushrooms and celery in 2 tablespoons butter and 1 tablespoon oil until soft. Add bread crumbs and seasonings and mix well. Place ¼ egg and 1 tablespoon stuffing on each piece of pounded veal and roll up. Fasten with a round toothpick.

Dredge birds in flour and shake off excess. Brown birds slowly in remaining oil and butter, and place in an ovenproof dish, seam side down. Deglaze pan with brandy and pour over birds. Add consommé and enough white wine or sherry to cover. Birds should just fit in pan. Cover, bring to boil, and bake at 350° one hour.

Five minutes before serving, beat sweet cream into sour cream (this keeps it from curdling) and add to casserole. Heat through and serve very hot with rice. Remove toothpicks.

*Serves 4*                    —MRS. JAMES W. RILEY, JR.


2   tbsp. salad oil
1   medium onion sliced
2   lbs. veal stew meat cut in 1" chunks
1   tbsp. chopped parsley
salt and pepper
12  oz. beer (1 can)
½   cup chopped celery
1   carrot sliced
½   lb. mushrooms, sliced
1   cup sour cream

# VEAU DE LA CAMPAGNE

Heat oil in large kettle. Add onions, parsley and seasonings. Cook until meat is browned, turning occasionally. Add beer, celery and carrots. Cover and simmer until meat is tender—about 1½ hours. Add mushrooms during last 15 minutes of cooking. Remove from heat, stir in sour cream.

*Serves 6*                    —MRS. BAYARD WALKER

# BRAISED VEAL SHANKS IN MARJORAM SAUCE

2 tbsp. butter
2 tbsp. vegetable oil
3 veal shanks (5 to 6 pounds) cut in 2½-inch pieces
1 cup chopped onion (1 large)
1 large clove of garlic, minced
1 cup dry white wine
2 cans (8 ounces each) tomato sauce
2 tbsp. dried marjoram, crumbled
1 tsp. salt
dash of pepper
2 tbsp. chopped parsley, stems reserved

Heat butter or margarine and oil in kettle or heavy saucepan over medium heat. Add shanks; brown on all sides. Remove from pan; reserve. Add onion to fat left in pan. Cook 5 minutes, stirring occasionally. Return shanks to pan. Add garlic, wine, tomato sauce, marjoram, salt, pepper, and parsley stems. Bring to boiling. Cover. Reduce heat. Simmer 1 hour to 1 hour and 15 minutes or until meat is tender.

Remove shanks to serving dish with slotted spoon. Correct seasoning of sauce. Strain over meat. Sprinkle with chopped parsley.

*Serves 4 to 6*                         —IRENE BALLLENGER

2   lbs. boneless shoulder of veal
2   tbsp. flour
1½  tsp. salt
½   tsp. pepper
½   tsp. paprika
¼   cup butter
1   cup onion, finely chopped
2   cloves garlic, minced
2   tsp. fresh or ½ tsp. dried tarragon
1   tbsp. fresh parsley
1½  cups chicken stock
1   tbsp. Dijon-style mustard
½   cup slivered Brazil nuts
2   tbsp. butter
chopped parsley to garnish

# TARRAGON VEAL

Cut the veal in 1½″ cubes, coat in flour and seasonings, and brown in butter, in a skillet, one layer at a time. Remove veal and sauté onion and garlic in remaining butter. Return veal to skillet, sprinkle with tarragon and parsley, add stock, and simmer covered for one hour or until tender.

Using a slotted spoon, transfer the veal to a heated serving dish and keep warm. In a small bowl stir one cup of hot broth into the mustard. Add the Brazil nuts which have been sautéed in the remaining butter and pour over veal. Garnish with more chopped parsley. If you serve this dish with rice, flavor the remaining broth with more mustard and pass it separately.

*Serves 6*                —MRS. WILLIAM F. YOUNG

*Tarragon*
The Herball

# STUFFED VEAL BREAST

1 veal breast, 3 to 4 lbs.
1 onion
4 ribs celery
1 tbsp. butter
4 slices white bread
8 leaves sage or 1 tbsp. dried, crushed
salt and fresh-ground pepper
1 cup cream
1 carrot, sliced
1 cup rich chicken broth, or more

Cut a pocket above the bones of the veal breast to hold the stuffing. Mince together the onion and celery. A food processor is wonderful for this. In a skillet, cook the minced vegetables in the butter to soften them slightly. Make the bread into fine fresh crumbs and add the crumbs and shredded sage leaves, and quite a lot of salt and pepper to the vegetables. The stuffing should be spicy. Remove the pan from the heat and moisten the contents with some of the cream. Put the stuffing in the pocket of the veal, close the opening.

Slice the carrot and put it in the bottom of a roasting pan. Lay the veal breast, bones down, on the carrot. Sprinkle on salt and pepper, pour on 2 tablespoons of cream and 1 cup of broth. Cover pan tightly with foil and bring to a boil on top of stove. Bake at 350° for 1 hour. Test meat to be sure it is very tender. If so, remove the foil and brown the meat lightly under the broiler.

Remove the veal breast to a heated platter and keep warm. Scrape the contents of the roasting pan into a blender or food processor. Puree the solids and pour all into a saucepan. Stir in the remaining cream and reduce the mixture slightly. Coat the veal with a little of the sauce and pass the rest.

Serve by carving the veal in slices between the bones. If you like liver, ½ pound of diced, fresh chicken livers added to the stuffing is delicious.

*Serves 4 to 6*                    —HANNAH M. RHODES

## VEAL PIE

2  *cups left-over cooked veal*
½  *cup bread crumbs or 1 cup left-over stuffing*
*salt, pepper*
1  *tbsp. chopped parsley*
½  *cup diced mushrooms*
1  *onion, minced*
½  *cup veal gravy or broth*
1  *egg*
1  *pie shell*

Chop veal roughly and mix with the crumbs, salt, pepper, parsley, mushrooms and onion. Pour into a 9-inch pie pan. Beat the gravy into the egg and pour over the meat. Moisten the rim of the pie pan, lay the pie crust on top, and seal the edges with a fork. Brush the top with a little milk, slit it in several places, and bake at 350° about 40 minutes until the crust is golden brown.

*Serves 6*                              —MARY AMBROSE

# PRESSED VEAL

1 cracked veal knuckle
1 lb. boned shoulder of veal
8 cups water
2 carrots, peeled
1 stalk of celery, scraped
6 peppercorns
3 bay leaves
small bunch of parsley
salt
2 tbsp. unflavored gelatin
4 hard boiled eggs
lemon juice

Simmer the knuckle and veal in the water with the peppercorns, bay leaves and parsley stems and 2 tsp. salt 1½ hours, skimming the surface froth as it rises. Add the carrots and celery and simmer ½ hour more. Remove the meat, carrots and celery and strain the liquid through a fine sieve. Return the liquid to the pot and reduce it to 5 cups. Add more salt if needed. It will taste less salty when it is cold.

Sprinkle gelatin over ⅓ cup cold water and soften 5 minutes. Stir into hot broth until thoroughly dissolved. Cool aspic to lukewarm. Mince the veal. Slice the carrots, celery and eggs thinly. Chop parsley leaves.

Rinse 8-inch long loaf pan in cold water. Pour in a thin layer of aspic and chill until it sets. Arrange slices of egg, carrot and celery in a decorative pattern on the aspic. Sprinkle with parsley and carefully spoon aspic over your design. Chill. Add ½-inch layer of veal, sprinkle with salt, pepper and lemon juice, and a lot of parsley. Spoon over aspic and chill. Continue layering ingredients until all are used up, then chill at least 3 hours. Serve inverted on a chilled platter garnished with parsley.

*Serves 8*
          —ALIDA HAYES

4   *lamb or venison kidneys*
4   *slices fried bacon*
½  *pint sour cream*
1   *teaspoon Worcestershire*
*savory, thyme*
*salt and pepper to taste*

# KIDNEYS, HUNTER STYLE

Buy very fresh, young kidneys. Soak in cold water for several hours. Slice extremely thin and dip in flour. Fry bacon for garnishing. Then use hot fat to sear kidneys on both sides for a minute or two. Remove to a warm platter; place in warming oven. In fat remaining in frying pan, stir sour cream, Worcestershire, savory, thyme, and other seasonings. If too thick, thin with sweet cream. Pour sauce over kidneys. Serve at once.

*Serves 2*
      —MRS. WALTER PAUL PAEPCKE

De tuenda bona valetudine

# VEAL HEART SAUTÉ

1    veal heart
2–3  tbsp. fat from the heart (or oil)
2    tbsp. butter
4    mushrooms, minced
1    onion, minced
1½   tbsp. flour
½    cup canned tomatoes
1    glass sherry
chopped parsley
salt and pepper

Cut the heart in thin slices, removing the veins. Lightly salt and pepper slices and sauté in very hot fat or oil until browned on both sides but still pink inside. Remove meat and keep warm. Pour fat from pan and melt butter in it. Cook the mushrooms and onion until the onion is golden. Mix in the flour and cook 2 more minutes. Add the tomatoes and bring to a boil. Add the sherry and parsley to taste. Return the meat to the pan and stir, but do not boil anymore. Serve meat and sauce in a ring of white rice.

*Serves 2*                        —DAVID PACE

1   smoked tongue (beef)
1   onion, sliced thin
2   tbsp. butter
1   heaping tbsp. flour
2   cups boiling water
¼   cup vinegar
½   cup tomato catsup
¼   cup raisins
3   bay leaves
salt and sugar to taste
pepper (black) and cayenne to taste

# EMILY HENROTIN'S MARMADUKE TONGUE

Boil smoked tongue until tender; skin and slice. Sauté onion in butter. Add flour and mix well. Add water gradually, stirring. Add vinegar, catsup, raisins, bay leaves, salt, sugar, and peppers. Simmer 15 minutes. Add tongue slices. Simmer another 15 minutes. Serve hot. (For plenty of sauce, double recipe.)

Serves 4                          —LIZA FOSBURGH

*To make a Mothes Powder to lay amongſt your Linnen or Wollen Clothes*

Take the moſs of a ſweet apple tree lay it in ſteep in roſe water all one night ſtop the veſſel very cloſe that it is in then lay it a drying in a paper in a warme oven So ſteep it and dry it 3 times then beat it very fine and put to the powder of cloves the powder of ſweet marjerom orace powder damaſke powder as much muſk and ambergreeſe as you pleaſe no civit for that will clam it then put it in a taffety bag ſo uſe it.          —BOOK OF SIMPLES

# SWEETBREAD CASSEROLE

1 pair sweetbread
white wine and water to cover (about 2 cups each)
5 tbsp. butter
1 cup bread crumbs
1 hard boiled egg
salt and fresh-ground pepper
1 tbsp. minced chives
3 tbsp. flour
1 cup chicken broth
1 cup milk

Simmer the sweetbread in the wine and water for 20 minutes, dunk into ice water, remove tendons and skin, and slice ¼ inch thick. Cover the bottom of a lightly buttered baking dish with the bread crumbs. Arrange the sliced sweetbread over the crumbs. Dice the egg white and sprinkle it on. Then sprinkle on the mashed yolk, salt, pepper, and chives.

Cook together 3 tablespoons of the butter and the flour for 3 minutes. Add gradually the chicken broth and then the milk. Stir until thick and season with salt and pepper. Pour sauce over the sweetbread, dot with remaining butter, and brown under the broiler.

*Serves 4* —MRS. WILLIAM C. STEERE

2   pairs sweetbreads (2 lbs.)
2   tbsp. lemon juice
water, salt
2   cups cooked ham, cubed
4   tbsp. butter
1   green pepper, sliced
½   lb. fresh mushrooms, sliced
1   tbsp. flour
¼   tsp. pepper
1   clove
1   cup heavy cream
½   cup dry sherry

# SWEETBREADS AND HAM IN SHERRY

Simmer sweetbreads for 20 minutes in two quarts water to which has been added the lemon juice and 2 tsp. salt. Remove and plunge in cold water. Remove membrane and veins and cut sweetbreads into cubes.

Melt butter in a large heavy saucepan. Add green pepper and sauté five minutes or until tender. Add mushrooms and sauté until tender. Stir in flour, ½ tsp. salt, pepper and clove and cook flour 2 minutes. Stir in sherry and then cream, then add ham and sweetbreads as mixture thickens. Simmer 8 to 10 minutes to heat through and blend flavors. Do not boil. Serve on toast.

*Serves 6*                                    —ALIDA HAYES

*Clove*
**The Herball**

# Pasta & Rice

# MACARONI TUNA SALAD

1 box (12 oz.) corkscrew macaroni
1 tbsp. olive oil
3 cups broccoli florets
7 oz. canned tuna
2 or 3 anchovy fillets or more
1 cup mayonnaise
2 tbsp. capers
juice of ½ lemon

Cook macaroni al dente, drain, toss with olive oil, and chill. Blanch or steam the broccoli until it is barely cooked, drain, and chill in ice water to preserve the color. Several hours before serving toss the macaroni, broccoli, tuna in chunks, and chopped anchovies gently. Stir the mayonnaise, capers, and lemon juice together and toss with the salad. Chill to blend flavors.

*Yields 6 entree servings* —ROBERTO DeVIRA

*Broccoli*
The Herball

½    *lb. cooked and cooled elbow macaroni*
1    *green pepper sliced*
1–2  *tomatoes cut into wedges*
3    *hard-boiled eggs, cut into wedges*
2    *celery stalks, chopped*
1    *chicken breast*
*salt and pepper to taste*
1    *cup mayonnaise*

# GRANDMA'S OWN MACARONI SALAD

Cook chicken in enough water to cover. Add salt and pepper and celery tops for flavor. When chicken is cooked through let cool and cut into bite-sized pieces. Place in large bowl. Strain and reserve broth.

Combine all other ingredients with the chicken. Mix thoroughly. Loosen mayonnaise with some of reserved broth (1 to 2 tablespoons) and add to other ingredients, mixing thoroughly to coat all. Adjust salt and pepper to taste. Chill thoroughly before serving. One dish meal or for party buffets.

*Serves 6*

—ANN ROGENER

# GNOCCHI di POLENTA BIANCA

1 quart milk
1 cup butter
1 cup hominy grits (not "quick" grits)
1 tbsp. salt
pepper
1 cup grated Gruyère cheese
⅓ cup grated Parmesan cheese

Cut ½ cup butter into pieces, add it to the milk in a very large heavy saucepan, and bring the milk to a boil. Stir while pouring the grits into the milk in a thin stream. Add the salt and pepper, reduce heat, simmer and stir constantly until the milk is absorbed. Cover the pan and let it sit in a warm spot for 10 minutes.

Turn the grits into a mixing bowl and beat with a mixer at medium speed for 5 minutes. Pour the grits into a 13 × 9 × 2 inch dish, cover, and chill until set or overnight. Cut the set mixture into 12 rectangular pieces and arrange them, overlapping, in a shallow baking dish that can be brought to the table. Melt the remaining ½ cup butter and pour it over the gnocchi. Sprinkle on the Gruyère and then the Parmesan cheese. Heat at 400° for 30 minutes and serve hot.

*Serves 6* —MRS. WILLIAM C. STEERE

8   oz. taglialette (very thin, ½ inch wide, noodles)
4   oz. sweet butter
8   oz. cheese, grated (Parmesan, Gruyère or mixed)
2   tbsp. flour
1½  cups milk
grated nutmeg to taste
pinch powdered cloves
cayenne pepper to taste
½   tbsp. tomato puree
2   garlic cloves, minced
3   eggs + 1 egg white

# TAGLIALETTE SOUFFLÉ

Generously butter a 2½-quart soufflé dish Dust with some of the cheese (preferably Parmesan). Cook 2 ounces of butter and flour together 3 or 4 minutes without browning. Remove from heat and slowly beat in the milk, then the nutmeg, clove, pepper, and tomato. Cook until thick and smooth. Remove from heat and let stand while you cook the pasta al dente and beat the egg whites stiff.

Toss the drained pasta with the remaining butter, and the garlic. Beat the egg yolks, one at a time, into the sauce. Stir in all but 1 tablespoon of the cheese. Fold in the egg whites, and gently mix in the pasta. Pour into the soufflé dish, top with the remaining cheese, and draw a circle on top. Place in a 400° oven and bake 20 minutes. Reduce heat to 350° and bake 20 to 25 minutes more until the top is well browned and crusty. Serve with spinach salad dressed with sweet basil vinaigrette.

Serves 4                           —MRS. FREDERICK P. HOUSTON

*Pepper*
De plantis epitome utilissima

# MIKE'S RIGATONI

1 lb. Italian sausage (sweet)
3 tbsp. oil
1 clove garlic, minced
1 onion, chopped
1 lb. fresh mushrooms, sliced
1 bay leaf
salt and pepper to taste
1 6 oz. can tomato paste
2 cans water
1 lb. rigatoni
½ cup grated Parmesan

Cut sausage into 1-inch pieces. In a large skillet, heat oil and brown sausage well. Add garlic, onion and mushrooms; sauté for 10 minutes. Add bay leaf, salt and pepper; blend in tomato paste and water. Cover skillet and simmer for 1 hour. Cook rigatoni, drain well and place in a baking dish. Remove bay leaf; pour sauce over rigatoni, mix well; sprinkle on Parmesan, and bake at 350° for 10 minutes until top is lightly browned.

*Serves 6* —EILEEN K. SCHOFIELD

*Bay Leaf*
The Herball

1  cup minced parsley
2  shallots, minced
¼  cup butter
½  cup dry white wine
1  lb. bay scallops
¾  cup heavy cream
¾  cup milk
1  cup grated Romano cheese
salt, pepper, fresh-ground
12  oz. fresh green fettuccini noodles

# FETTUCCINI WITH PARSLEY AND SCALLOPS

In a large, heavy saucepan cook half the parsley and the shallots in the butter until the shallots are soft. Add the wine and reduce by half. Stir in the scallops until well mixed, add the milk and cream and simmer 5 minutes. Meanwhile, throw the fettuccini into a large pot of boiling water and cook just to barely done (al dente). Remove sauce from heat and stir in the cheese. Stir in the parsley, salt, pepper, and nutmeg. Arrange the drained fettuccini on a platter and pour the sauce over it.

*Serves 4*

—HOLLAND VOSE

*Mrs. Hellen Parrys Receipte for a Cold*

Take ye faireſt orange you can get roſt it at ye fire then put thereto a pretty quantity of Sallet oyle ſweeten it with Sugar candie or Sugar drinking it 1st in ye morning & laſt at night.

—BOOK OF SIMPLES

# FETTUCCINI WITH CHICKEN LIVERS AND MUSHROOMS

1     *lb. chicken livers, cut in ½" pieces*
½     *cup butter*
½     *lb. mushrooms*
⅔     *cup onion, minced*
½     *cup dry vermouth*
1½  *cup heavy cream*
1     *cup tomatoes, peeled, seeded, and chopped*
*sugar, salt, pepper to taste*
1     *tbsp. fresh or 1 tsp. dried basil, chopped*
1     *tsp. fresh or pinch dried rosemary, chopped*
1     *lb. fettuccini*
*parsley, chopped*
*Parmesan cheese*

In a heavy skillet, sauté livers in some of the butter, just long enough to brown the outsides. Centers should be pink. Remove livers, add mushrooms and onions to skillet and butter as needed. Cook 2 to 3 minutes. Raise heat to high, add vermouth, and boil away all the liquid. Stir in the cream, tomatoes, and seasonings and reduce by ½. (If using fresh herbs, wait to add them until after sauce is reduced.) Return livers to sauce and stir in.

Toss fettuccini, cooked al dente with remaining butter (about 2 tbsp.), and cover with sauce. Top with Parmesan cheese and minced parsley, and more basil if it is fresh. Toss at table before serving and pass more Parmesan.

*Serves 4 to 6*

—MARY HOMANS

*Wheat*
Commentarii

2   to 3 cups cooked, cold rice
1   can (7 oz.) tuna fish
1   tart apple, grated, cored, and chopped
3   ribs celery, sliced
½   cup pecans, coarsely chopped
½   cup raisins
¼   cup olive oil
2   tbsp. wine vinegar
salt and pepper
parsley

# R I C E   S A L A D

Toss the first six ingredients together to mix. Add the oil and toss again, then the salt and vinegar and toss again. Chill overnight. Before serving, taste and correct seasonings. Toss with some chopped parsley. Garnish with more parsley and fresh-ground pepper.

*Serves 4*                         —SHAREN BENENSON

1   cup raw rice—cook until tender
1   cup chopped chiles
2   cups sour cream
½   pound Monterey Jack cheese, grated

# M E X I C A N
# R I C E

Mix sour cream and chiles. Butter a casserole and add alternate layers of rice, sour cream and chiles. Salt and pepper each layer. Top layer should be sour cream. Dot with butter and grated sharp cheese. Bake in 350° oven, about 30 minutes, until brown.

*Serves 8*                    —MRS. WILLIAM F. YOUNG, JR.

# CAJUN RED BEANS AND RICE

½ pound dried pinto, kidney or pink beans
1 quart water
¼ pound salt pork, diced
1 cup chopped onions
½ cup chopped green pepper
1 clove garlic, crushed
1 tsp. each *fresh oregano and thyme leaves*
2 tsp. salt
1 can (8 ounces) tomato sauce
½ pound well-seasoned pork sausage meat, crumbled
½ cup sliced green onions with tops
3 cups hot cooked rice

Sort and wash beans. In a large saucepan combine beans, water and salt pork. Bring to a boil and boil 2 minutes. Remove from heat and let stand, covered, 1 hour. Return to heat and simmer 45 minutes. Add onions, green pepper, garlic, seasonings, and tomato sauce. Continue simmering, covered, 45 minutes, stirring occasionally. Stir in sausage and green onions; replace cover and cook 30 minutes longer or until beans and sausage are tender. Add boiling water if beans become dry while cooking. Serve beans with mounds of fluffy rice.

*Serves 6*                                    --AIMÉE JONES

7    cups broth
2    tbsp. butter
2    tbsp. oil
½    cup chopped onion
2    cups white Italian rice
½    cup dry white wine
½    tsp. saffron
2    tsp. salt
4    tbsp. soft butter
½    cup grated Parmesan cheese
fresh-ground pepper

# RISOTTO ALLA MILANESE

In a separate pan, bring the broth to a simmer and keep it simmering slowly. In a wide heavy skillet melt the butter in the oil and sauté the onion until it is soft. Add the rice and stir until it becomes transparent. Add the wine. One cup at a time, add the hot broth and stir and simmer until it is nearly absorbed. When half the broth is used, add the saffron and salt to the rice and continue stirring in the broth. When the last cup of broth has begun to be absorbed stir in the remaining butter and then the cheese. The mixture should be creamy and the rice still firm. The total cooking time is about 25 minutes. Add salt and pepper to taste and serve hot.

*Serves 4 to 6*                    —ROBERTO DeVIRA

*Crocus (Saffron)*
The Herball

## GREEN RICE

2 cups cooked rice
1 medium onion, grated
¼ cup butter
1 large bunch parsley, minced
½ cup grated cheddar cheese
½ cup milk
salt and pepper

Sauté the onion and rice in the butter until they are golden. Toss with the parsley and most of the cheese and salt and pepper. Pour into a buttered baking dish, pour over the milk, and sprinkle on the remaining cheese. Bake at 350° for 20 to 30 minutes. This is wonderful with ham, turkey, etc.
*Serves 4 to 6*                    —MARGARET RYAN

## DATE AND ALMOND PILAF

3 cups cooked rice
½ cup pitted, chopped dates
½ cup raisins
2 onions, diced
½ cup chopped parsley
¾ cup roasted almonds
salt and pepper
1 tbsp. water

Toss all ingredients together until well mixed in a 2-quart covered casserole. Cover tightly and heat at 350° for 20 to 25 minutes.
*Serves 6*                    —MRS. JOHN A. BROWN, JR.

1   *garlic clove*
2   *tsp. minced fresh ginger*
1   *tbsp. butter*
2   *tbsp. salad oil*
1   *or 2 thin pork chops*
6   *shrimp*
½  *cup chopped scallions, including tops*
4   *cups cooked rice, at least 1 day old*
2   *eggs*
*salt and pepper*
*cucumbers, tomatoes, and more scallions*

# THAI FRIED RICE

Mash the garlic clove and cook it and the ginger in the oil and butter in a deep, heavy skillet for 30 seconds. Slice the pork into very thin strips, add to the skillet and stir-fry over high heat until cooked through. Stir in the shrimp, cut in ½-inch pieces, and the scallions, and stir until the shrimp turn pink. Stir in the rice and cook until it is heated through. Scrape the mixture to the sides of the pan leaving a 5-inch circle of the skillet's bottom bare. Break the eggs into this circle. Add salt and pepper and stir the eggs to scramble them. When they are softly set, stir them up with the rice mixture.

Mound the fried rice on a platter and garnish with fresh cucumbers, tomato, and more scallions.

*Serves 4*           —ROBERTO DeVIRA

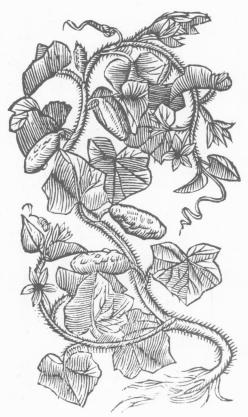

*Cucumber*
Theatrum Botanicum

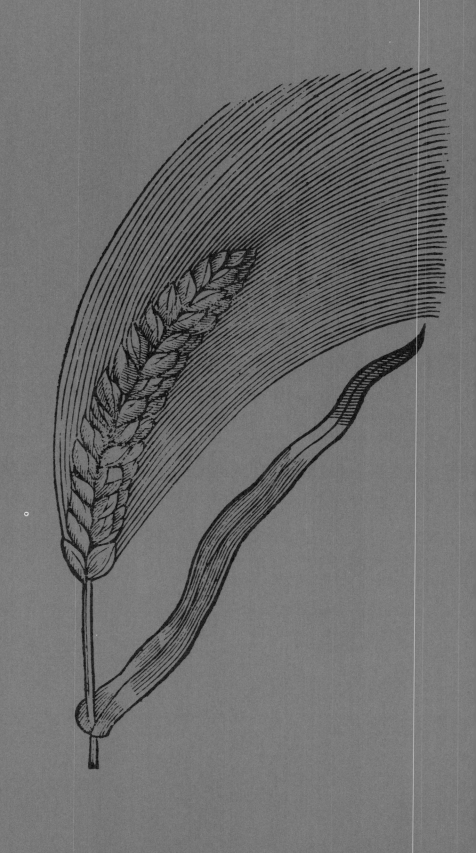

*Breads*

# CLAUDIA'S BREAD

2 pkgs. dry yeast
½ cup warm water
3½ cups hot water
1 cup oatmeal
½ cup flaxmeal
½ cup wheat germ
1 cup whole millet
½ cup sunflower seeds
2 tsp. salt
2 tbsp. oil
⅓ cup molasses
1 cup honey
4 cups whole wheat flour
5 cups unbleached white flour

Dissolve yeast in the ½ cup warm water and let cool. Combine the oatmeal, flaxmeal, wheat germ, millet, sunflower seeds, and salt. Stir in 3½ cups very hot water and the oil, and let mixture cool. Stir in the molasses and honey and the yeast mixture.

Using your hands work in the whole wheat and white flours. Knead dough well, return to bowl and let rise 1½ to 2 hours until double in bulk. Punch down and divide into 4 loaf pans. Let rise to top of pans. Bake at 350° for 40 to 45 minutes. *Yields 4 loaves*

—MYRA MATHERS

*Sunflower*
The Herball

¼    cup butter
3    cups sifted flour
2½   tsp. baking powder
½    cup sugar
1¼   cup buttermilk
½    tbsp. caraway seeds
¼    cup raisins

Cut the butter into the flour, baking powder, and sugar. Add 1 cup of buttermilk and mix well. Add enough more buttermilk to make a sticky dough. Use your hands to mix it. Work in the seeds and raisins. Place the ball of dough in a greased, 9 inch iron skillet, cover with a domed lid or mixing bowl the same diameter and bake over low heat on top of the stove or in the coals of a fire for 1 hour or so until bread tests done with a skewer.

*Yields 1 loaf*                    —MRS. LANGDON SIMONS

*Tester's note:* This works fine on top of the stove, although the bottom may char. It may also be baked in a loaf pan at 350° for 1 hour and stored to "mellow" for two days before serving. It is an excellent breakfast bread.

# STOVE TOP
# IRISH BREAD

*Caraway*
Theatrum Botanicum

## IRISH BROWN BREAD

2   cups sifted unbleached flour
1   cup sifted whole wheat flour
1   cup wheat germ
2   heaping tsp. baking powder
1   level tsp. baking soda
3   tbsp. sugar
½   cup butter, melted
1¾  to 2 cups buttermilk

Stir the dry ingredients together in a bowl. Stir in the butter and then the buttermilk. The mixture should be wet enough to form into a ball but not too soft to knead.

Knead the bread on a flour covered board until it is smooth and elastic. Form into a loaf or a ball and place in a greased and floured bread pan or round 9″ pan. Bake at 350° for 1 hour and 10 minutes. When bread is done it will sound hollow when thumped on top.

If you wish a soft crust, cover the bread with a damp dish towel when you remove it from the oven and cool it in the pan. If not, turn the bread out of the pan shortly after removing it from the oven and lightly butter the top.

*Yields 1 loaf*

—IRENE McDOUNELL

3    cups boiling water
1½   cups regular oatmeal
¾    cup molasses
1    tbsp. salt
⅓    cup butter or margarine
2    pkgs. active dry yeast
½    cup warm water
½    cup unprocessed bran
½    cup wheat germ
2    cups whole wheat flour
4    to 5 cups white flour

# OATMEAL BREAD

Pour boiling water over oatmeal. Add molasses, salt and butter, and cool. Soften yeast in warm water. Add to oatmeal mixture. Beat in bran, wheat germ and flours gradually to make a firm dough. Knead well on a floured board until smooth and elastic (8 to 10 minutes). Roll in a greased bowl to coat, cover bowl, and let rise until double in bulk (1½ hours). Punch down, knead again (2 to 3 minutes). Divide dough. Makes 4 small or 3 medium sized loaves. Place in greased pans. Let rise until double in bulk (¾ to 1 hour). Bake at 350° about 40 minutes.
*Yields 3 or 4 loaves*                    —MARIAN W. LEES

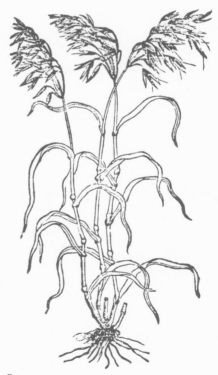

*Oats*
The Herball

# OLIVE-NUT BREAD

2½ cups all-purpose flour
4 tsp. baking powder
½ cup sugar
1 egg
1 cup milk
½ cup butter or margarine, melted
1 cup sliced green olives (stuffed with pimiento)
1 cup chopped walnuts

Sift dry ingredients into a large bowl. In a small bowl, beat egg, stir in milk and gradually add melted butter. Pour mixture into dry ingredients and stir until well blended; gently stir in olives and nuts. Spoon dough into a greased 9 × 5 loaf pan. Bake at 350° for 60 minutes, until bread tests done in center. Cool 10 minutes in pan, remove to rack and cool completely. Serve with cream cheese, toasted, if you like. This bread slices better the second day.

*Yields 1 loaf* —EILEEN K. SCHOFIELD

*Olive*
The Herball

| 1     | cup instant rolled oats |
| 1½    | cups boiling water      |
| 1     | cup white flour         |
| 1     | tsp. cinnamon           |
| ½     | cup walnuts             |
| 1½    | cups sugar              |
| 1     | tsp. baking soda        |
| ½     | cup oil                 |
| 1     | tsp. vanilla            |
| 2     | eggs                    |

# OATMEAL TEA BREAD

Pour water over oats and stir. Set aside. In a large bowl stir together the flour, cinnamon, walnuts, soda, and sugar. Add the oil, oats, and vanilla and beat at low speed until mixed. Beat at medium speed 2 minutes, scraping the bowl. Add the eggs and beat 2 more minutes. Pour into a greased and floured loaf pan and bake at 350° for 1 hour and 10 minutes until a tester comes out clean.

*Yields 1 loaf*

—ANN BROOKS

*A Powder to make the Teeth White and Sweet*

*Take the powder of Sage the Shavings of ivory put them amongft ye juice of lemons & every evening and morning rub your teeth therewith & it will make them both white and fweet.*

—BOOK OF SIMPLES

# MANDEL BREAD

2   *eggs*
¾   *cup sugar*
¼   *cup mayonnaise*
1½  *cup flour*
1   *tsp. baking powder*
1   *tsp. vanilla*
1   *cup chopped prunes and raisins*
½   *cup nuts*
*cinnamon to taste*

Use an electric beater to combine the eggs, sugar and mayonnaise. Mix the flour and baking powder, after it has been sifted. Add to first mixture and beat well by hand. Add vanilla, raisins, prunes and nuts. (Dough will be soft.)

Grease cookie sheet and make 2 strips of the dough. Sprinkle cinnamon over forms and bake at 350° about ½ hour. When done, cut into slices and refrigerate.

Chopped fruit or chocolate bits may be substituted for raisins and nuts.

*Yields 2 loaves*        —HARRIET FRANK

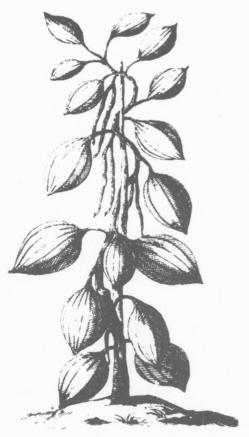

*Vanilla*
Histoire Generale des Drogues

1½   *sticks butter*
2    *cups sugar*
4    *eggs*
1    *cup milk*
*grated rind of 2 lemons*
3    *cups flour*
2    *tsp. baking powder*
½    *tsp. salt*
2    *cups chopped walnuts*
*juice of 2 lemons*
½    *cup sugar*

# LEMON
# BREAD

Cream the butter and 2 cups sugar. Add, and continue beating, the eggs, milk, and grated rind. Sift together the flour, baking powder, and salt. Add them gently to the batter. Stir in the nuts. Divide batter among three small, well greased loaf pans and bake at 350° for 60 minutes. The top of the loaves should be split when done. Mix the remaining ½ cup sugar and lemon juice and heat to dissolve the sugar. Pour over the loaves immediately after removing them from the oven. Cool the loaves in the pans. Good sliced thin for tea.

*Yields 3 loaves*                    —MRS. C. E. ROCKWELL

## GRANDMA'S RASPBERRY MUFFINS

1 egg
½ cup milk
¼ cup vegetable oil or melted shortening
1½ cups sifted flour
½ cup sugar
2 tsp. baking powder
½ tsp. salt
1 cup fresh raspberries

Heat oven to 400°. Grease muffin tin. Beat egg slightly with fork. Stir in milk and oil. Sift dry ingredients together and stir until flour is moistened. *Batter should be lumpy.* Do not overmix. Add fruit, mix lightly. Fill cups ⅔ full. Bake 20 to 25 minutes. Loosen immediately with a spatula.
*Yields 12 muffins*   —MRS. WILLIAM F. YOUNG, JR.


## PRUNE BREAKFAST RING BREAD

2 cups scalded milk
2 tbsp. butter
2 tsp. salt
2 tbsp. sugar
2 eggs
2 pkgs. dry yeast
15 oz. box dried, pitted, prunes
1 scant cup whole wheat flour
1 cup rye flour
4 cups white flour

While the milk is hot, stir in the butter, salt and sugar. When mixture cools, stir in the eggs and mix well. Sprinkle the yeast over the top and let it dissolve. Let stand about 15 minutes while you snip the prunes in small pieces with scissors. Stir the prunes and liquid together in a large bowl and work in the flour. (6 cups of white flour may be used instead of the combination.) Cover and let rise to double in bulk.

Punch the dough down and on a lightly floured board shape into two rings to bake on a cookie sheet. You can also pinch off pieces the size of walnuts and place them, sides touching, in 2 greased ring molds. Let rise about an hour to double in bulk. Bake at 350° for 45 minutes.

*Yields 2 breakfast rings*     —LIZA FOSBURGH

# APPLE MUFFINS

3½  *cups flour*
1¾  *cups sugar*
1    *tsp. salt*
1    *tsp. cinnamon*
1    *tsp. soda*
1½  *cups cooking oil*
3    *eggs*
3    *cups finely chopped apples*
1    *cup chopped nuts*

Combine ingredients in order listed and mix well. Pour into greased and floured muffin tins and bake at 350° for 10 to 15 minutes for tiny muffins. Full-size muffins take 25 to 30 minutes to bake. Loaf pans bake in 1 hour. Raw dough may be stored in the refrigerator for 1 week.
*Yields 60 tiny muffins or 2 loaves*

    —MRS. MICHAEL SLATER

## ROSEMARY BISCUITS

2    *cups unbleached flour*
3½ *tsp. baking powder*
*pinch of salt*
2    *tbsp. sweet butter*
1    *egg*
*milk*
1    *small sprig minced rosemary*

Sift flour, baking powder, and salt together. Cut in the butter and rosemary. Beat the egg in a measuring cup, and add milk to make ¾ cup liquid. Add the liquid to the dry ingredients until the dough is easily handled. On a floured board fold the dough over itself 6 times and roll it out ½ inch thick. Cut biscuits. Place a dot of butter on each and bake at 450° for 15 minutes. These are delicious with tea, wine, or to end a meal. *Yields 18 to 20 biscuits*

—MRS. FREDERICK P. HOUSTON

## SWEET POTATO BISCUITS

3    *medium sweet potatoes*
2    *tbsp. butter*
½    *cup sugar*
¼    *cup milk*
1½ *to 2 cups flour*
2    *tsp. baking powder*
½    *tsp. salt*

Boil the sweet potatoes, peel, and mash them, and measure out 1½ cups for this recipe. Stir the butter into the warm potato and then the sugar and milk. Sift together 1½ cups flour, the baking powder, and salt, and combine with the potato mixture. When thoroughly blended, the dough should be stiff enough to roll out. If not, add more flour until it is.

Roll dough out 1 inch thick and cut into biscuits. Bake, not quite touching, on an ungreased cookie sheet, for 20 minutes at 350°. These are wonderful with ham on a buffet table.

*Yields 2 to 2½ dozen* —MRS. LEWIS A. CLARKE

## ZEPHYRS

1   *cup white corn meal*
1   *tbsp. lard*
1   *tsp. salt*
4   *cups boiling water*
4   *egg whites*
⅛   *tsp. salt*

Scald the meal, 1 teaspoon salt, and lard with the boiling water. Cook it in the top of a double boiler ½ hour, stirring frequently. Cool to room temperature. Beat the egg whites with ½ teaspoon salt until stiff. Fold into the meal. Drop from a spoon onto a greased cookie sheet and bake 35 minutes at 350°. These are a nice change from rolls or biscuits served with ham or other roasted meat.

*Yields 2 dozen zephyrs* —MRS. J. HENRY HARPER

# POTATO FLOUR ROLLS

4   eggs, separated
½   tsp. salt
pinch cream of tartar
1   tbsp. sugar
½   cup potato starch
1   tsp. baking powder
2   tbsp. ice water

Beat the egg whites stiff with the salt and cream of tartar. Beat the yolks with the sugar until they form a ribbon. Sift the potato starch with the baking powder and add to the yolks alternately with the ice water. Fold in the whites and pour into lightly buttered muffin tins. Bake 15 to 18 minutes at 350°. These taste like very light brioche. Serve with butter and jam.

*Yields 12*

—SHAREN BENENSON

Sponge:

*1   package yeast, dissolved in ¼ cup tepid water*
*½  cup sugar (double for cinnamon rolls)*
*2   cups tepid milk (I use ½ cup non-fat dry milk + water to make 1 pt.)*
*2   cups bread flour*

Mix and let rise in a warm place until doubled in bulk.

Dough:

*1   tbsp. salt*
*3½ cups unbleached flour*
*½  cup salad oil*

Stir down sponge and then stir in salt, flour, and oil in several additions. Form into a ball in the bowl, oil the top, and allow to rise again until double in bulk. Part of dough may now be frozen for later use. (I freeze 2 pkgs. of ⅓ each and thaw it in the microwave oven set on "defrost" for one minute.)

Roll dough out on floured surface, cut to size, brush with butter and fold in half. Let rolls rise to double on baking sheet and then bake at 400° until golden brown. Approximately 68 calories each if tops are not brushed with butter.
*Yields 6 dozen 2" rolls*
—ELINOR SOUTHERLAND

# GRANNY CHISHOLM'S YEAST ROLLS

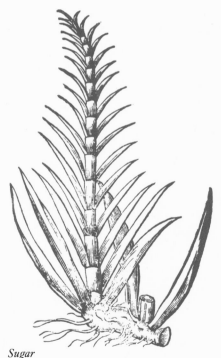

*Sugar*
The Herball

155.

# TANSEY CAKES

2 cups flour
½ tsp. baking soda
½ tsp. salt
2 eggs
½ cup molasses
1 cup milk
2 tbsp. butter, melted
½ cup earliest tansey sprouts
big pinch cream of tartar

Sift together the flour, baking soda, and salt. Separate the eggs, and combine the yolks, molasses and milk. Beat this and the melted butter into the flour. Chop enough of the top 1 inch of the first tansey sprouts to make ½ cup. Stir this into the batter. Beat the egg whites with the cream of tartar until they hold peaks. Fold them into the batter. Drop from a soup spoon onto a hot, oiled, griddle. These silver dollar-size pancakes make a wonderful early spring breakfast.

*Serves 4 to 6* —MRS. HENRY STANLEY

1   egg
1   cup milk
1½  cups sifted unbleached flour
½   tsp. salt
2   tsp. sugar
⅓   cup corn oil
3   tsp. baking powder

# GRAND-MOTHER'S WAFFLES

Beat the egg lightly and then beat in the milk. In a larger bowl, stir together the flour, salt, and sugar. Gradually stir in the eggs and milk, and then the oil. Let stand at least 15 minutes. Just before using, sprinkle the baking powder over the batter and beat it in well. It's easier to use a pitcher to pour the batter on a hot waffle iron. *Yields 7 seven-inch waffles*

—MRS. CHARLES G. PROFFITT

*Tester's Note:* These days when most waffles are made with pancake mix and are puffy things with soft middles, these are as satisfying to chew as al dente pasta and are just crisp crusts with no "middle" at all.

*For Deafnefs*

*Put ground Ivy one leafe into each ear rowle it up but not too hard put it in frefh morning and evenings.*
—BOOK OF SIMPLES

# Hot Vegetables

# SWISS POTATO CAKE WITH BACON

1½  lb. potatoes
salt and pepper to taste
3    tbsp. minced fresh parsley
½    tsp. dried basil
1    garlic clove, crushed
3    tbsp. butter
2    tbsp. vegetable oil
½    cup grated Parmesan
2    slices crisp cooked bacon

Put scrubbed potatoes in cold water, bring to boil, simmer for 10 minutes or until barely tender. Drain and cool and chill for at least 2 hrs. Peel the potatoes and grate them coarsely (there should be 4 cups grated). Sprinkle with salt and pepper and stir in herbs.

In a 7-inch omelet pan or iron skillet heat 2 tablespoons butter and 1 tablespoon vegetable oil. Add the potatoes and tamp down and tidy edges. Cook the cake for 7 minutes without stirring until bottom is browned and crisp. Invert cake on to a plate, add 1 tablespoon butter and 1 tablespoon oil to pan. Slide cake back into pan with uncooked side down. Cool for 7 minutes. Turn cake onto flameproof plate, sprinkle with grated cheese and crisscross bacon on top with more cheese. Melt cheese under preheated broiler.
*Serves 3 or 4*                         —FAITH H. McCURDY

## MAINE SALT POTATOES

*very small new potatoes—red or white*
*iodized or sea salt*
*butter to taste*

Place the potatoes (5 to 6 per serving) in a heavy casserole and cover with water. Add enough salt to float a raw egg in its shell and cook until tender. Test with fork—potato should be soft but not mushy. Drain. A white coating of salt should appear on each potato. Dab with butter and serve.

—S. DORSEY SMITH

## KALE AND POTATOES

2   *lbs. kale*
2   *lbs. potatoes*
4   *tbsp. butter*
½   *cup milk*
*salt and pepper to taste*

Wash kale thoroughly and then separate green leaves from midrib by just pulling, or stripping. Cover with water and cook until tender. Put by thirds into a blender and with off and on motion until appearance is similar to chopped spinach.

Cook and mash potatoes. Mix with kale and add lumps of butter—or any meat gravy you may have. Then add about ½ cup of milk after the above mixture has heated through.

*Serves 6 to 8*
                                —B. ELIZABETH WUNDER

# SPINACH BARS

1 cup flour
1 tsp. salt
1 tsp. baking soda
2 eggs
¼ cup melted butter
½ cup chopped onion
1 pkg. frozen chopped spinach
1 lb. sharp cheddar cheese
Parmesan cheese

Sift together the flour, salt, and baking soda. Beat the eggs lightly and add them and the butter to the flour. Add the onion and the thawed, drained spinach. Shred the cheese, add it, and mix well. Spread in a well-greased 8 × 11-inch baking pan. Sprinkle with Parmesan cheese. Bake at 350° for 45 to 60 minutes until nicely browned and crusty. Cut into small squares.

*Serves 8 to 10* —MRS. HENRY B. GUTHRIE

*Spinach*
Flora Danica

4   medium potatoes
4   tbsp. oil
1   or 2 cloves garlic, minced
½   tsp. powdered ginger
1   tbsp. powdered coriander
dash cayenne pepper
salt to taste
1   lb. spinach

## INDIAN SPINACH AND POTATOES

Peel potatoes and cut into quarters. In a large skillet, heat oil and brown the potatoes; add spices and sauté for 5 minutes. Wash spinach and chop coarsely. Add spinach to potato mixture and mix well. Cover skillet and simmer until potatoes are tender, about 15 minutes; add a bit of water if necessary.
Serves 4

—EILEEN K. SCHOFIELD

2   packages frozen, chopped spinach
1   cup heavy cream
2   eggs
salt, pepper, nutmeg
¼   cup grated Parmesan
2   tbsp. butter

## GRATINEED SPINACH RING

Thaw and drain the spinach well. Mix with cream, lightly beaten eggs, salt, pepper, and nutmeg to taste. Pour into a heavily buttered ring mold or bread pan. Sprinkle on cheese and dot with butter. Bake at 350° for 30 minutes or until set. Turn out on a warm plate.
Serves 4 to 6

—MRS. BURNHAM BOWDEN

## GLOIRE TURNIPS

2 lbs. turnips
3 tbsp. butter
⅓ cup heavy cream, whipped
2 tsp. rum
3 tbsp. dry sherry
salt and pepper
pinch of celery seed
4 oz. grated cheese

Boil turnips, peel when just tender, and mash well. Stir in all the other ingredients including 2 ozs. of cheese. Place in a buttered soufflé dish and top with the remainder of the cheese. Place in oven at a low heat for five to ten minutes. This was my mother's favorite with game and beef.
*Serves 4 to 6*          —MRS. FREDERICK P. HOUSTON

## CRISP VEGETABLE SAUTÉ

2 tbsp. butter
1 clove garlic, crushed
1 carrot, cut like matchsticks
1 small turnip, cut like matchsticks
1 onion, sliced and divided in rings
1 red pepper, cut in strips
1 cup broccoli florets (or cauliflower)
salt and pepper
1 tbsp. chopped basil

Melt the butter and sauté the garlic and vegetables 4 or 5 minutes, stirring often. Season with salt and pepper to taste. Scatter the basil on top and serve.
*Serves 4*          —REGINA F. BERENBACK

1  eggplant
3  tbsp. vinegar
4  tbsp. soy sauce
1  clove garlic
½  tsp. black pepper
minced scallion
handful Chinese parsley
2  tbsp. sugar
2  tbsp. sesame oil
2  slices ginger root (minced)
½  tsp. "hot" oil
1  tsp. salt

# CHINESE EGGPLANT

Boil eggplant whole and unpeeled until done. Cut in half and turn down to drain and cool. Mix sauce and pour over cut sides. Refrigerate overnight. Next day cut into slices, and serve.

*Serves 4 to 6*
　　　　　　　　　　　　—LOUISE MORO

*For very ſtrong Fitts or Fitts in Great People*

Take the outlandiſh ſingle piony roots and cut off yᵉ outſide of them ſlice them as thin as poſſible and dry them juſt enough to be made into fine powder give to a child as much as will lye on a 2 pence and to a great body twice as much 3 days before the full and 3 days after the ſame time before and after the change in a ſpoonfull of black cherry water and at any time if the fits be ſtrong you may give it after the fit is juſt over and give 2 ſpoonfulls of the water after it.

　　　　　　　　　　　　—BOOK OF SIMPLES

# BAKED EGGPLANT

*2 eggplants*
*1 cup bread crumbs*
*1 tbsp. chopped parsley*
*1 tbsp. olive oil*
*2 cups tomato sauce, see below*

Slice eggplants obliquely about ½ inch thick. Plunge into boiling salted water and cook for 3 minutes. Drain thoroughly. Arrange on a flat dish, lightly oiled. Spread each slice thickly with a tomato sauce, made as follows.

Sprinkle with bread crumbs and chopped parsley and pour over a few drops of olive oil. Cook uncovered in a 325° oven about one hour.

Tomato Sauce

*1 shallot*
*1 lb. tomatoes*
*1 tsp. minced parsley*
*1 tsp. shredded basil*
*salt, pepper*
*sugar to taste*

Cook a finely chopped shallot or small onion in a mixture of oil and butter. Add 1 lb. roughly chopped, ripe tomatoes or 1 can tomatoes, a little parsley and basil. Season with salt, pepper and a bit of sugar. Simmer until thick. Put through a food mill. If too liquid, return to pan and allow to dry over a gentle heat.

*Serves 4 to 6*
—ALICE GREER

1  medium size eggplant
salt and pepper
1  beaten egg
2  tbsp. melted butter
1  small onion chopped
1  cup dried bread crumbs
1  pint stewed (canned) tomatoes
2  or 3 shallots, chopped
¼  cup Parmesan cheese

# SCALLOPED EGGPLANT

Pare eggplant and cut 1 inch cubes. Cook in water until tender; drain thoroughly. Add salt and pepper to taste. Add egg, butter, onion, shallots and bread crumbs. Mix thoroughly and place in greased baking dish. Place layer of tomatoes on top. Sprinkle with bread crumbs and Parmesan cheese to cover. Bake in moderate oven (375°) for about 30 minutes.

*Serves 6*
—ELEANOR B. BELL

4  slices bacon
½  cup sliced mushrooms
½  cup sliced scallions
⅛  cup sesame seed
1  large head chicory, chopped
pepper to taste

# STIR-FRIED CHICORY

In a large skillet, cook bacon until crisp; place on paper towels to drain. In bacon fat, sauté mushrooms and scallions for 5 minutes. Add chicory and sesame seed; cook and stir for 5 min., until sesame seed is golden and chicory is slightly limp. Crumble bacon on top, sprinkle with pepper and serve at once.

*Serves 4*
—EILEEN K. SCHOFIELD

# ONION PANADE

1½ lb. large sweet *Bermuda* or *Spanish onions,*
   *thinly sliced*
*salt to taste*
¼ *cup butter*
8 *ounces dried-out Italian or French bread*
   *sliced into ⅓-inch thick slices (about 24*
   *slices)*
1½ *cups freshly grated Parmesan*
1½ *cups freshly grated Swiss Gruyère*
*lightly salted boiling water*
*grated Parmesan or Gruyère*
*stick of hard butter*

Place onions, salt and butter in heavy pan. Place over very low heat, using a Flame Tamer if necessary. Cook covered for 40 minutes, then removing cover, cook, stirring occasionally for another 20 minutes until the onions take on a rich caramel color.

In a deep 4 quart casserole spread ⅓ of the bread slices, cover with ½ the onions. Sprinkle with ⅓ of the grated cheese mixed together. Add ⅓ more of the bread, the remaining onions and another ⅓ of the cheese.

Top with the remaining bread and cheese. The casserole should only be ⅔ full at this point. Ease the tip of a funnel down the side of the casserole and pour in boiling salted water slowly until the bread level rises 1 inch or until it is just floating. Cook on top of the stove, uncovered, over low heat, to maintain a slow bubble for 1 hour.

Preheat the oven to 350°. Again add boiling,

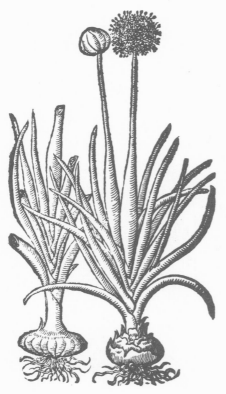

*Onion*

Theatrum Botanicum

168.

salted water, using a funnel, just to float the top bread. Add a little more cheese on the surface. Shave paper-thin slices of butter all over the top. Bake 1 hour. After 40 minutes, check to see whether the top is forming a crust of gratin. If not, increase the oven heat by 25 to 50 degrees.
*Serves 4 to 6*                              —FAITH H. McCURDY

# DILLED ZUCCHINI AND POTATOES

*4 small zucchini*
*4 onions*
*2 potatoes*
*2 to 3 tbsp. minced dill*
*2 tbsp. olive oil*
*salt and pepper*

Trim and scrub the zucchini, peel the onions and potatoes, and slice them all thinly. Lightly oil the bottom of a heavy skillet. Cover it with a layer of zucchini and salt and pepper lightly. Add a layer of onions and one of the potatoes, sprinkle on dill and a little oil. Repeat until vegetables are all used. Cover and let stand a few minutes before cooking so that the salt can draw out some liquid from the zucchini. Cook slowly on top of the stove about 30 minutes until vegetables are done. Sprinkle some more minced dill on top before serving.
*Serves 4*                              —LIZA FOSBURGH

*Dill*
Kreuterbuch (Roselin)

# BUTTERNUT SQUASH

2 large butternut squash (choose ones with long necks)
⅓ cup heavy cream
½ cup sour cream
¼ lb. oleo or butter
1 tbsp. allspice
salt and pepper to taste

Bake squash in 325° oven for about an hour or until a knife when inserted in neck of squash goes in easily. Save necks of squash and discard the rest. Peel and mash and add other ingredients. Stir and heat slowly.

Serves 6 —MRS. DONALD J. BRUCKMANN

# RED CABBAGE

1 head red cabbage
1 onion
¼ tsp. caraway seeds
1 tbsp. brown sugar
3 tbsp. vinegar
2 tbsp. vegetable oil
salt and pepper

Slice cabbage very fine; chop onion. Heat 2 tablespoons vegetable oil in large kettle and add cabbage and onion. Sauté, stirring often for 10 to 15 minutes, on medium low fire. Add caraway seeds. Add brown sugar and vinegar, cover and cook over low fire until tender—about 40 minutes. Stir from time to time and check that there is enough liquid in the pot; if not, add a tablespoon or two of water. Season to taste with salt and pepper. This should stand for a day to develop flavor.

Serves 6 to 8 —SALLY GOODMAN

1½ lbs. green beans
¼ lb. mushrooms
½ cup chopped celery
4 tbsp. butter
3 tbsp. flour
1 cup milk
salt and pepper
1 can water chestnuts or 8 Jerusalem artichokes
1 can fried onion rings

# GREEN BEAN CASSEROLE

French-cut the beans and steam them 10 minutes. Sauté the mushrooms and celery in a tablespoon of butter until they are wilted, and add them to the beans. Make a white sauce of the remaining butter, flour, milk, and salt and pepper to taste. Slice the water chestnuts and toss them with the beans, etc., and white sauce. Pour into a buttered casserole and bake at 350° for 20 minutes. Top with the can of onion rings and bake 5 minutes more.

*Serves 6 to 8*                        —WILHELMINA ALLEN

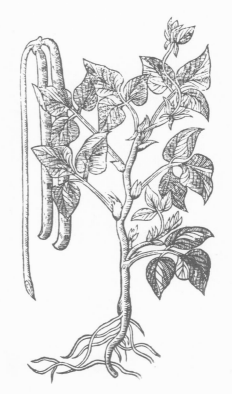

*Bean*
Theatrum Botanicum

## HERBED BROCCOLI

1  large bunch broccoli
2  cups chicken broth (canned)
¼  cup chopped onion
1  bay leaf
1  tsp. marjoram
¼  tsp. thyme and celery seeds
springs of parsley
3  tbsp. melted butter

Wash broccoli, trim off ends of stalks. Cut large stalks in half. Blend all other ingredients except butter. Bring to a boil, add broccoli and cook, covered, until just tender. Drain well, pour melted butter over it and serve.
*Serves 4*
—ELEANOR ISDALE

## CELERY ROOT TIMBALES

8  celery roots
5  eggs, separated
salt and pepper to taste
2  tbsp. butter

Peel and trim roots, boil for about 20 minutes until soft. Drain and rub through a sieve or food-mill. Blend in yolks, season with salt and pepper, fold in beaten egg whites. Fill buttered timbale molds with the mixture, place in a pan with hot water, and bake at 325° for about 20 minutes or until firm.

Serve around pheasants or bake in a ring mold and fill center with peas.
*Serves 10*
—PHYL MALLORY

2 *lbs. carrots, peeled and cut into narrow 2-inch long strips*
*water*
2 *tbsp. butter*
2 *tbsp. brown sugar*
2 *tbsp. brandy*

In a saucepan, cook carrots in water until just tender; drain well. Add other ingredients, stir and cook over low heat until carrots are glazed. *Serves 6*            —EILEEN K. SCHOFIELD

# BRANDIED CARROTS

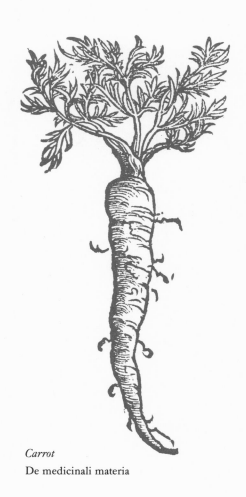

*Carrot*
De medicinali materia

## OYSTER PLANT
(Salsify)

2 bunches oyster plant
4 tbsp. butter
1 pint cream
½ lemon (juice of)
chopped chives
salt and pepper to taste

Scrape and cut up oyster plant in small pieces, dropping each piece into bowl of cold water with juice of ½ lemon. This is to prevent discoloration. Drain and cook in boiling salted water for 25 minutes. Drain and add butter. Let simmer for 15 minutes, allowing butter to absorb. Add cream and simmer slowly for 25 minutes. Stir gently several times. Add chopped chives, salt and pepper to taste just before serving.
*Serves 4*     —MRS. LAWRENCE McKEEVER MILLER

## SAUTEED CUCUMBERS

4 cucumbers
salt
2 tbsp. butter, approximately
1 tbsp. chopped basil

Select nice young straight cucumbers that are not seedy. Peel the cucumbers and halve; cut each half into six long wedges. Put in a flat dish and sprinkle with salt. Leave for about 30 minutes. Drain cucumbers and put in a skillet with melted butter to cover the bottom of the skillet. Try to cook only a single or slightly overlapping layer at once. Sauté over medium heat until just tender (5 minutes or so, depending on heat),

174.

turning gently as you cook (do not break up).
Remove to a heated platter and sprinkle with
fresh basil. Serve at once. If doing more than one
layer, keep cooked cucumbers in warm oven
while you do rest. Don't sprinkle with basil until
ready to serve. (Needs no extra salt).
*Serves 4*                           —LIZA FOSBURGH

*3 cucumbers*
*1 tbsp. butter*
*1 cup milk*
*1 tbsp. flour*
*2 tbsp. cream*
*1 scant tbsp. vinegar*
*1 egg yolk*
*salt and pepper to taste*

Peel 3 cucumbers and cut lengthwise in quarters
and remove seeds. Cook in salted water 20 minutes. Blend butter, milk, flour, and cream over
low heat. Add vinegar, salt and pepper. Add egg
yolk just before serving and pour over drained
cucumbers.
*Serves 4*                    —MRS. DONALD B. STRAUS

*Cucurbit*
The Herball

# JERUSALEM ARTICHOKES AND MUSHROOMS

*2 lbs. Jerusalem artichokes*
*1 pound mushrooms*
*1 cup milk*
*2 tbsp. flour*
*3 tbsp. butter*
*salt and pepper*

Boil artichokes in salted water until soft and then peel. Peel mushrooms and sauté in butter. When mushrooms are golden, add artichokes. Sprinkle with flour and add milk, stirring until smooth. Add salt and pepper to taste and serve when well blended. Can be kept in double boiler.
*Serves 4* —MRS. JOHN G. WINCHESTER

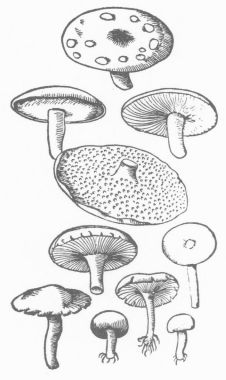

*Mushroom*
De plantis epitome utilissima

3  tbsp. butter
1  lb. thinly sliced mushrooms
2  tsp. fresh lemon juice
2  tbsp. finely chopped green onions
salt and pepper to taste
½  cup milk
½  cup heavy cream
¼  tsp. nutmeg
2  tbsp. flour
⅓  cup bread crumbs
⅓  cup grated Swiss cheese

# MUSHROOMS AU GRATIN

Heat half the butter in 1 quart saucepan and add mushrooms and lemon juice. Cover closely and simmer until mushrooms have wilted and given up most of their juices. Add chopped onions, salt, pepper, milk and cream and bring to a boil. Season with nutmeg. Knead flour with remaining butter. Add it bit by bit to mushroom mixture, stirring. When sauce is thickened pour creamed mushrooms into heatproof dish and sprinkle with mixture of bread crumbs and cheese. Brown under broiler. Serve hot.
*Serves 4 to 6*
—SYLVIA STEIN

*For the Megrime in the Head*

*Take goates dung and mix it with vinegar of fquils and anoint the head and temples therewith. or this, frankinfence mirrh and an egg beat them together & apply it to the head and temples.*
—BOOK OF SIMPLES

# Cold Vegetables & Salads

# COLE SLAW

1   large head of cabbage
2   medium onions
⅓   cup chopped parsley
1½  tbsp. vinegar
¾   cup mayonnaise
2   tbsp. dijon mustard
1   tsp. sugar
1   tbsp. celery seed
1½  tsp. salt
freshly ground pepper

Shred cabbage and onions in a food processor using the slicing blade. Turn into a large mixing bowl and add the chopped parsley. Sprinkle on the vinegar and toss lightly. In a separate bowl mix the mayonnaise, mustard, sugar, celery seed, salt and pepper. Pour over the cabbage, toss well, and chill. Serve in a lettuce-lined glass bowl. Delicious with almost any entree . . . most especially, fish.

*Serves 8*                     —MRS. GARDNER COWLES

# BROCCOLI ORIENTAL

1 bunch of broccoli
3 tbsp. salad oil
1 tsp. sesame oil
2 tbsp. rice vinegar
1 tbsp. soy sauce
fresh-ground pepper

Cut apart broccoli florets. Scrape the stems and cut them in 1-inch by ½-inch pieces. Steam the broccoli lightly. It should still be crisp. Toss with the other ingredients and chill.

*Serves 4*                     —MRS. ROBERT CARLETON

180.

1   head cauliflower
½   cup mayonnaise
½   cup sour cream
2   tsp. Dijon mustard (or more to taste)
handful chopped fresh mint or 1 tbsp. dried
salt and pepper to taste

## CAULIFLOWER SALAD

Cut and break cauliflower into bite-size pieces. Simmer in salted water until barely cooked. It should be very firm. Drain and cool the pieces to room temperature or chill.

Combine the rest of the ingredients and toss with the cauliflower before serving. If using dried mint, prepare the dressing a day before and refrigerate to allow the flavor to develop.

*Serves 4 to 6*

—MARY HOMANS

1   lb. small okra pods
1   small onion
½   cup mild white vinegar
½   cup water
½   tsp. red pepper flakes, or more
salt to taste

## OKRA GUADELOUPE-STYLE

Cut the caps off the okra and slice the onion in thin strips, lengthwise. If okra is longer than 2 inches, cut it in 1 inch slices. Combine with other ingredients in a covered saucepan and let stand for 1 hour, stirring occasionally. Bring to a boil and simmer 5 minutes until okra is barely tender. Serve at room temperature or chilled.

*Serves 4*

—AIMÉE JONES

# FOUR BEAN SALAD

2   cups cooked string beans
2   cups cooked wax beans
2   cups cooked kidney beans
2   cups cooked white beans
⅓   cup olive oil
3   tbsp. vinegar
½   tsp. dry mustard
1   tbsp. sugar
1   tsp. salt
fresh-ground pepper

Fresh string and wax beans and home cooked kidney and white beans are best, but canned are quite acceptable. Peas may be added or substituted. Drain all the beans and cut the string and wax beans in 1-inch pieces. Toss to mix. Mix the mustard, salt, and sugar, shake with the oil and vinegar, and pour over the beans. Refrigerate in a glass container at least 24 hours, mixing occasionally, before serving.

*Serves 8 to 10* —MARY CAMP BENENSON

*Bean*
Theatrum Botanicum

1½  cups dry pea beans
3   large cloves garlic
½   cup olive oil
2   to 3 tbsp. vinegar
salt and pepper
1   large garden tomato
1   green pepper
parsley or watercress

# ARMENIAN WHITE BEAN SALAD

Soak the beans in water 2 or 3 hours or over-night. Drain and place in a heavy saucepan. Add 1 teaspoon of salt and fresh water to cover the beans by at least one inch. Bring to a boil and simmer until tender. Don't overcook them.

Peel the garlic and put it in a tight-lidded container large enough to hold the beans. Use very large pieces of garlic and leave them whole so that they're easy to remove later. Add the drained, hot, beans and ¼ cup oil. Cover the container and allow the beans to cool slowly, turning and shaking gently from time to time to coat beans with oil. When they reach room temperature, refrigerate the beans.

When ready to serve, chop the tomato and the pepper in ½-inch pieces. Remove the garlic from the beans. Pour them in a serving bowl and arrange the tomato and pepper on top. Sprinkle on salt and grind on black pepper. Mix the remaining ¼ cup oil with the vinegar and pour it evenly over all. Garnish with roughly chopped parsley or watercress.

Serves 6

—SHAREN BENENSON

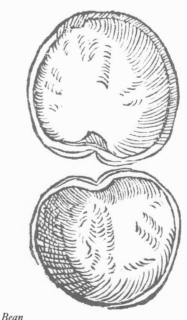

Bean
Theatrum Botanicum

# LENTIL SALAD

2 cups dry lentils
2 dill pickles
1 to 2 tbsp. pickle juice
2 oz. tin of anchovies
4 scallions
½ cup olive oil, approximately
2 to 3 tbsp. vinegar
salt and pepper
parsley

Rinse the lentils and simmer them in salted water until they are just tender. Drain and toss gently with ¼ cup oil. Cool. When they reach room temperature, add the coarsely chopped pickles, anchovies, and scallions. Add the pickle juice and anchovy oil and toss. Add more oil if necessary and vinegar to taste, and toss. Refrigerate. Just before serving, toss and taste. Add salt if necessary and grind in fresh pepper. Toss again and serve garnished with chopped parsley.

*Serves 6 to 8* —SHAREN BENENSON

1  *large eggplant*
1  *very small onion*
¼  *to ⅓ cup olive or corn oil*
2  *tbsp. milk*
*pepper and salt to taste*

Take the whole eggplant and place it over a high open flame of a gas stove (or in the oven at 500°) and let it bake on both sides till it simmers inside the skin. The process of baking it should be fast for preventing the oxidation (darkening) of the flesh.

After simmering a few minutes, take it off the flame and let it cool down then peel the skin rinsing your fingers very often in a bowl of cool water; hold the flesh with both hands under a slow jet of cool water and rinse it thoroughly then let it drain down on an inclined chopping board. When very well drained, detach the peduncle and put the eggplant in a mixer together with the finely chopped onion, milk, oil, salt and pepper and mix it a few minutes, then whip it for about 1 to 2 minutes.

Dump the eggplant paste on a wide plate, flatten it with a spatula and decorate with slices of half of a tomato.

*Serves 6*
—DR. FLORITZA DIACONESCU

# EGGPLANT SALAD

# FARMERS BOUNTY SALAD

(A good recipe for the processor)

1 cup shredded cabbage
1 cup diced cucumbers
1 cup sliced radishes
1 cup chopped green pepper
1 minced onion
4 fresh tomatoes, cut in pieces
salt and pepper—a sprinkle

Place all ingredients in a bowl and toss with Sour Cream Dressing.

Sour Cream Dressing

1   cup sour cream
2   tbsp. vinegar
1   tbsp. sugar
1   tsp. salt
1   tsp. dry mustard
½   tsp. paprika

Add vinegar and seasonings to sour cream. Blend well and pour over the salad. Toss gently. (This dressing will keep for a week or so.)

—DOROTHY GREENLEE

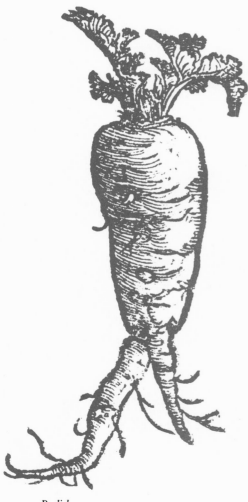

*Radish*
Kreuterbuch (Roselin)

1  lb. shelled peas or 2 pkgs. frozen peas, thawed
1  cucumber
3  tbsp. crushed mint
1  tbsp. chopped chives
1  tbsp. lemon juice
½  cup mayonnaise
½  cup sour cream
1  tsp. sugar
½  tsp. salt

# COOL MINT PEAS

Peel, seed, and chop the cucumber. Toss in a bowl with the peas, mint, and chives. Whisk together the remaining ingredients and toss with the vegetables.

*Serves 4*                    —VIRGINA CAPORALE

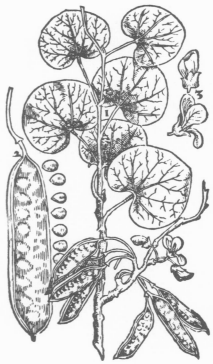

*Pea*
De plantis epitome utilissima

## SWEET AND SOUR SPINACH SALAD

1 10-oz. pkg. fresh spinach, torn in pieces
1 can water chestnuts, sliced
1 can bean sprouts, drained
2 hard boiled eggs
5 strips fried bacon, crumbled

Dressing

¾ cup sugar
1 cup salad oil
1 small onion, diced
3 tablespoons Worcestershire sauce
⅓ cup catsup
¼ cup vinegar
¼ tsp. salt

Blend in food processor or blender and toss with salad.
*Serves 8*
—MRS. WLLIAM F. YOUNG, JR.


## MOROCCAN CARROT SALAD

1 lb. raw carrots
1 clove garlic
1 tsp. cumin seed
salt to taste
¼ tsp. cayenne pepper
¼ cup olive oil
juice of ½ lemon, or more

Shred the carrots. Mince the garlic and sprinkle it and the cumin and salt and pepper over the carrots. Pour the oil and lemon juice evenly over all and toss. Refrigerate overnight to blend the flavors. Add more salt and lemon juice if necessary before serving.
*Serves 6*
—SHAREN BENENSON

6   cucumbers
2   tsp. salt
3   tbsp. white wine vinegar
½   tsp. sugar
1   clove garlic, crushed
2   tbsp. tomato paste
¼   cup olive oil
1   cup sour cream
salt and pepper
3   tbsp. fresh dill, chopped

# FINNISH CUCUMBERS

Peel and slice the cucumbers as thinly as possible. Place in a bowl and sprinkle with salt, sugar, and 1 tablespoon of vinegar. Let stand 1 hour at room temperature.

Combine the garlic, tomato paste, oil and sour cream and remaining 2 tablespoons vinegar in that order. Drain the cucumbers well and toss with the dressing. Chill. Add dill and salt and pepper and toss again just before serving.

*Serves 8*                                —ANNALEE OSBOURNE

*Cucumber*
Commentarii

# BLUE CHEESE AND BACON POTATO SALAD

3 lbs. new potatoes
⅓ cup dry vermouth
⅓ cup chicken broth
2 tbsp. minced parsley
2 tbsp. minced scallion
¼ lb. bacon
2 tbsp. or more white vinegar
salt and pepper
8 oz. blue cheese

Steam the potatoes in their jackets until tender. Quarter the potatoes while still warm and toss with the wine, broth, parsley, and scallions. Cool to room temperature. Fry the bacon crisp, crumble it, and pour it and its fat over the potatoes. Toss. Add vinegar and salt and pepper to taste. Toss again. Just before serving, crumble in cheese and toss again. Serve chilled or at room temperature.
Serves 10 to 12

—S. DORSEY SMITH

1 lb. string beans
½ lb. potatoes
1 small red onion
1 clove garlic
¼ cup olive oil
½ cup white wine vinegar
2 tbsp. shredded mint or basil
salt and pepper

# MARINATED STRING BEAN AND POTATO SALAD

Snap the beans in ¾-inch pieces and simmer in salted water until tender. Drain and save ¾ cup of the cooking water. Boil the potatoes, cool, and cut in ½-inch cubes. Cut the onion in thin slices and make rings. Combine all ingredients including the cooking water and refrigerate 3 or 4 hours or overnight.

*Serves 6*

—ANN CAPOZZI

*An excellent Water to clear Hands and Face*

*Take a quart of fair water a pint of white wine the juice of 4 lemons put into thefe bean bloffoms elder bloffoms white lilly bloffoms a handful of them all put them amongft the wine and water and put into 4 wild dafie roots 4 marfh mallow roots and 2 or 3 bunches of wild tanfie as much of femitary the weight of 2 pence in campheer put all thefe together in an earthen pot fet the pot in warm aifhes all night then in the morning ftrain it through a piece of white cotton clean wafht and put it into a narrow mouth'd glafs fet the glafs in the fun 3 or 4 days in the heat of the fun if there be any rednefs or pimples in the face take the white dung of a hen and fo fteep it in that water all one night then ftrain it again through the cloth wafh your face with this water evening & morning if you wafh your hands with any of this water put thereto 3 or 4 bruifed almonds this is ye moft excellent water that ever was made to clear hands and face withall. Probatum Eft.* —BOOK OF SIMPLES

# Wildlings

# NETTLE (SPRING VEGETABLE)

*Nettle*
The Herball

*2 pounds of nettle tips*

Gather the tips of very young nettles, clip with scissors at the second leaf bracket. Never pick in flower.

Wash the nettle tips and cook them until tender in their own moisture.

Chop them roughly in their saucepan and stir in a large nut of butter. Cover, and when cool, place in refrigerator overnight.

Repeat the same process on the second and third day, and on the fourth day sprinkle on nettles a couple of teaspoons of lemon juice, a little salt and pepper, a *little* grated nutmeg, and brown sugar.

Reheat over low heat and serve dressed with a dollop of sour cream and freshly chopped parsley.
*Serves 4* —MRS. FREDERICK P. HOUSTON

Fiddleheads are the 5- to 6-inch long croziers of the ostrich fern (Matteuccia struthiopteris). They are delicious raw or cooked. The flavor is reminiscent of asparagus with lemon on it.

# FIDDLEHEADS

As many fiddleheads as you can gather without spoiling the ferns. Rub off the scales, rinse in cold water and chill in the refrigerator.

# RAW FIDDLEHEADS WITH DILL SAUCE

Dill Sauce

¾  *cup mayonnaise*
¾  *cup sour cream or yogurt*
*juice of ½ lemon*
¼  *cup finely chopped fresh dill or 2 tsp. dill seeds*
½  *tsp. sugar*
1  *tsp. salt or salt to taste*
1  *clove garlic, minced*

Mix and chill.

—LOUISE MORO

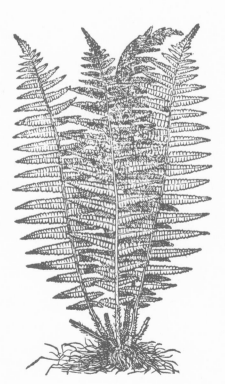

*Fern*
I discorsi

## FIDDLEHEADS WITH SOUR CREAM SAUCE

3 cups fiddleheads

Rub the scales off the croziers and rinse. Chop in 2-inch pieces, and simmer 5 to 8 minutes in salted water. Croziers should be crisp-tender.

Drain and toss in sour cream sauce.

Sour Cream Sauce

½   cup mayonnaise
½   cup sour cream
2   small dill pickles, chopped fine
3   tbsp. chopped parsley
2   tbsp. chopped chives

Mix and warm, but do not boil. Good with string beans, too.
Serves 4 to 6
—MRS. BURNHAM BOWDEN


## FIDDLEHEADS AND CAULIFLOWER SALAD

1   lb. fresh fiddleheads
¼   cup minced onion
½   cup salad oil
¼   cup good vinegar
2   tbsp. sugar
½   tsp. salt
fresh-ground pepper

Blanch the fiddleheads for about 2 minutes so they are still very firm. Drain and plunge in ice water to cool. Mix the rest of the ingredients and pour over the drained fiddleheads. Chill, stirring occasionally, overnight.
Serves 6
—ANNALEE OSBORNE

*2 cups fiddleheads chopped in 1" pieces*
*2 cups raw cauliflower broken in small pieces*

Blanch fiddleheads three or four minutes in salted water. Drain and chill in ice water. Drain again and dry. Toss with raw cauliflower florets in dill dressing.

### Dill Dressing

½   *cup mayonnaise*
½   *cup plain yogurt*
1   *tbsp. chopped fresh dill*
½   *tsp. salt*
½   *tsp. white pepper*

Mix well and toss with vegetables to coat them well. Refrigerate salad several hours to blend flavors.
*Serves 4 to 6*                    —MRS. C. VICTOR WILLIAMS

Clover (Trifolium) is also a delicious green. Here is a simple way to cook it.

C L O V E R

*fresh clover blossoms and young leaves*
*2  tbsp. butter to each pint of clover*
*salt to taste*

Melt butter in a heavy skillet, stir in clover and cook briefly over high heat until clover is barely wilted. Season to taste and serve. Allow one pint of clover for two servings plus one pint "for the pot."                    —MRS. HENRY E. COE III

## SPRING WEED SOUP

1 cup shredded weed leaves
·1 large onion
1 tbsp. butter
2 tbsp. rice
1 quart milk
1 egg yolk
½ cup cream
salt and pepper

Cook diced onion in butter until golden brown and put it in a double boiler with the rice and shredded leaves. Use a tightly-packed cup of shredded young dandelion, wild sorrel, lambs quarters, or best of all, a combination. Add milk (or half milk, half meat broth) and cook until rice is done. Stir the egg yolk into the cream and add to the soup. Heat 2 more minutes, season to taste and serve.

*Serves 4*                                    —MRS. WINSTON HAGEN

## CHICKEN DAY LILY SOUP

The flowers of the common orange day lily (Hemerocallis flava) grow wild along many roadsides. They are an exotic early summer treat. In order to prepare them for cooking, remove the pistil and stamens and rinse. Use only the petals, not the stem.

6 cups rich chicken broth
3 tbsp. rice
3 cups chopped day lily petals
salt and pepper to taste

Bring broth to boil and add rice. Simmer, stirring occasionally, 15 minutes. Add petals. Simmer three more minutes. Season to taste.

*Serves 4*                                    —JUDITH BECKWITH

3    shoulder pork chops
2    onions
1    clove garlic
1    tsp. salt
1    tbsp. soy sauce
1    tsp. ginger, minced
¼    tsp. sugar
1    tbsp. cornstarch
3    tbsp. peanut oil
1    tbsp. sweet white vermouth or sherry
½    cup water (or broth from boiled chop bones)
3    cups day lily (chopped flowers or whole buds)

Partially freeze meat. Slice into thin slivers leaving some fat on each piece if possible. Mash garlic and chop one onion finely. Cut the second onion in thin slices. Mix the meat, chopped onion, garlic, salt, soy sauce, ginger, sugar and cornstarch and let stand 15 to 20 minutes.

In a wok or large heavy skillet, heat oil until it starts to smoke. Immediately add meat mixture and stir constantly 3 to 4 minutes until meat is cooked. Reduce heat slightly if necessary to prevent burning, but it is important to keep mixture as hot as possible so that it is seared and doesn't give up all its liquid.

As soon as meat is browned, add vermouth and water and stir, then day lily and sliced onion and stir again. Cook another 3 to 4 minutes. The sliced onion should remain very firm. Serve immediately with rice.

*Serves 4*

—JUDITH BECKWITH

Commentarii

# FRIED DAY LILY BUDS

Whole, mature flowers, buds of day lily or pumpkin or squash blossoms are delicious prepared this way. It is really a Japanese tempura, so I have also given the recipe for tempura sauce.

4 *cups fresh day lily or other flowers*
*flour to dredge*
1 *cup flour*
*pinch of salt*
1 *tsp. sugar*
½ *tsp. baking powder*
1 *cup water*
1 *egg*

Mix the egg and water in one bowl and the dry ingredients in another. Then stir the wet into the dry, but leave the mixture slightly lumpy. Let sit in refrigerator at least 15 minutes. (You can leave it overnight or longer if you cover it, but it must rest at least 15 minutes.)

Rinse the flowers or buds, dredge them very lightly in flour, and lay them in one layer on a rack to dry. An oven shelf is useful here.

Heat at least 2 inches of oil in your widest skillet to 375°. At this temperature a drop of batter will sink to the bottom, remain there a second, then rise to the surface and sizzle gently. If it stays on the bottom, the oil is too cold. If it never sinks, just sizzles frantically on top, the oil is too hot. When frying the blossoms, try to maintain this temperature and your tempura will be light and greaseless.

De plantis epitome utilissima

Fry your tempura at serving time. Ideally you can do it in front of your guests in an electric skillet. Remove batter from refrigerator and stir gently. It should coat chopsticks or the handle of a wooden spoon and flow off in large drops. Add water in small amounts if batter is too thick. Dip each blossom in batter and lay it in the hot oil. Cook only 3 to 4 minutes until the crust is puffed and golden but the blosom is still firm. Chopsticks or a long handled fork can be used equally well to handle the blossoms. It is not necessary to turn them, but fry only one layer at a time and do not crowd pan.

Serve immediately on paper napkins with dipping sauce. You can make this into a main dish by adding butterflied, lightly pounded shrimp, cooked the same way, perhaps a minute longer. *Serves 6*

Dipping Sauce

| | |
|---|---|
| 1 | *cup chicken broth* |
| ¼ | *cup sugar* |
| ½ | *cup soy sauce* |
| 2 | *tbsp. dry sherry* |

Mix and put some in a bowl for each guest. Some people like their sauce sweeter with as much as twice as much sugar.

—ROBERTO DeVIRA

# PUFFBALL PIE

Wild mushrooms should never be eaten unless you are absolutely sure you have identified an edible species. You should not even touch them unless you can wash your hands immediately since some are so lethal they can make you very sick if a tiny residue is transferred to something else you eat.

Puffballs (Calvatia gigantea) are fairly easily identified, occur commonly, and are eaten by many people sautéed in butter. For those of you who are sure you know the puffball, here is a more sophisticated dish.

2   to 3 cups cubed puffball
4   tbsp. butter
2   tsp. dried thyme or 2 springs fresh
salt and pepper to taste
juice of ½ lemon
1   cup leftover meat, cubed
2   tbsp. butter
3   tbsp. flour
1   cup chicken broth
½   cup cream
¼   to ½ cup Madeira
1   pie crust
1   beaten egg

Slice puffball from top to bottom through center. Flesh should be solid and snowy white. If flesh is yellowing, or if there is any hint of a stem and unopened cap, throw it away and wash your hands. If not, cut the flesh in ¾-inch cubes.

*Puffball*
Theatrum Botanicum

Sauté the puffball in the 4 tablespoons butter for 10 minutes. While it is cooking, sprinkle on salt, pepper, lemon juice and thyme. Add meat at last minute to warm. Pour mixture into baking dish.

Cook the flour in the 2 tablespoons butter 2 or 3 minutes without browning in same pan. Stir in Madeira, then broth and cream and cook and stir until thickened. Pour into baking dish.

Cover with pie crust. Seal edges and brush with beaten egg. Slit the crust in a pretty pattern. Bake at 450° 15 minutes. Reduce heat and bake at 350° 10 to 15 minutes more until crust is golden.
*Serves 4*                              —SHAREN BENENSON

*fresh purslane*
*1 slice of bacon per person*

Having weeded out enough purslane (Portulaca oleracea) to feed your family, wash it, remove the roots, and chop it coarsely. In an iron frying pan, cook the bacon until crisp. Remove the bacon and put the purslane in the hot fat. Cook and stir briefly until the purslane wilts, crumble the bacon and mix it in. Then serve. The purslane has a nice "bite."

—MRS. HENRY E. COE III

# DELECTABLF PURSLANE

# MANICOTTI WITH EARLY SPRING LEAVES

12 manicotti
2 cups ricotta cheese
¼ lb. mozzarella cheese
1 egg
1 clove garlic
2 tightly packed, heaping cups chopped spring leaves; young dandelions, wild sorrel, watercress, lambs quarters, or a mixture
½ cup butter
½ cup cream
1 tsp. Worcestershire sauce, or more to taste
2 pimientos
¼ cup grated Parmesan cheese
salt and pepper

Cook the manicotti according to package directions. After draining them, put them in warm water to keep them flexible for stuffing. Meanwhile, mix the ricotta (you may substitute small curd cottage cheese), shredded mozzarella, and egg well. Crush the garlic and blend it and the leaves with the cheese. Season with salt and pepper and stuff the manicotti.

Place the stuffed manicotti in a lightly greased baking dish, barely touching. Melt the butter in the cream and season with Worcestershire sauce. Pour over the manicotti. Mince the pimientos and sprinkle on top. Sprinkle on the Parmesan and salt and pepper. Cover with foil and bake at 325° for 45 minutes.

*Serves 6*

—LIZA FOSBURGH

*Watercress*
The Herball

You can grow sorrel, of course, but over much of the Northeastern United States the wild sorrel, Rumex acetosa, appears in lawns and by the roadside. It can be substituted for the cultivated sorrel, Rumex scutatus, in any recipe, and is a particularly good foil for ricotta cheese in an omelet.

*2 to 3 tbsp. chopped sorrel*
*1 scallion, minced*
*1 cup ricotta cheese*
*salt to taste*
*freshly grated nutmeg to taste*

Mix all ingredients and let stand 15 minutes to blend flavors. Fill each omelet with 2 to 3 tablespoons of mixture. This is enough filling for 4 to 6 three-egg omelets. Since the sorrel is pungent, I leave people the option of grinding on pepper at the table.

—SHAREN BENENSON

# WILD SORREL OMELET

*Sorrel*
Theatrum Botanicum

# DANDELION SALAD

2 to 3 cups tender dandelion leaves
2 cups lettuce
4 slices bacon cut in ½" pieces
1 tbsp. flour
salt
pepper
½ cup milk
1 tsp. Dijon-style mustard
½ cup brown sugar
½ cup cider vinegar
¼ cup water
2 hard boiled eggs, chopped

Wash, dry and chill greens. Fry bacon crisp, remove bacon, reserve, and pour off all but 2 to 3 tablespoons fat. Stir flour into fat and cook until light brown. Remove from fire and stir in salt and pepper, milk, and mustard. Return to fire and cook until thickened. Gradually stir in sugar mixed with water and vinegar. Remove from fire. Stir in chopped eggs and bacon and pour over greens while still hot. Toss gently.
Serves 4
—DONNA STEVENSON

Dandelion
Theatrum Botanicum

3 *quarts dandelion blossoms*
4 *quarts water*
3 *pounds sugar*
2 *lemons*
1 *orange*
1 *cake yeast*

# DANDELION WINE

Collect fully opened blossoms as early in the day as the dew has dried. Put them, unwashed, into a large container, preferably glass or ceramic, but better metal than plastic. Boil the water and pour it over the blossoms. Let stand three hours without stirring.

Strain into a large pot and add the sugar and peels of the fruit. Bring to a boil, stirring until sugar is dissolved, then simmer 15 minutes. Cut the fruit into small pieces and put into a 2 gallon jar or crock. Pour the hot liquid with peels on top of the fruit.

Cool the mixture to 100° or body temperature. This takes a long time. Don't be impatient. When mixture is cool, dissolve the yeast in one cup of it and then stir the dissolved yeast into the rest of the liquid and let stand 12 hours.

Strain the mixture and return it to the cleaned crock or jar. Cover but do not seal. Let stand in a dark place two months. Strain into bottles and age six months more.

*Yields about 7 pints*

—MYRA MATHERS

Hortus Sanitatis

# SPRING SALAD

Mix together any of the following:

*Spinach (break into small pieces), chopped dandelion leaves, sliced fresh mushrooms, chopped chives, finely chopped scallions (particularly the green stalks), a little sliced apple, raisins, roasted nuts, and, if available, hop shoots. Great asset, if available, Paronychia—"chickweed" and Chenopodium album—"fat hen." Both of these weeds were greatly used by the Saxons. Chickweed, if cut constantly, will crop in delicate shoots until July.*

Dress with a sweet garlic vinaigrette, or try a sweet basil dressing:

3  *tbsp. chopped sweet basil*
4  *tbsp. good wine vinegar*
½  *cup olive oil*
1  *crushed clove garlic*
*pepper and salt*

Blend all together thoroughly, place in a jar and keep in a cool place—not cold. Allow to stand overnight before using.

—MRS. FREDERICK P. HOUSTON

*Chickweed*
Theatrum Botanicum

If you have one sassafras tree (Sassafras albidum) you will find every spring many unwanted saplings around it. When you pull these up you can use their roots. If you don't have your own tree, you can get almost as good results by using freshly picked leaves. (Dried, powdered leaves are also the essential gumbo ingredient "filé powder.") Dried roots may also be stored for year-round use.

Scrub young roots to remove dirt and chop in small pieces. Wash leaves.

*1 cup root or 2 cups leaves*
*4 cups water*
*sugar or honey to taste*

Simmer sassafras at least 10 minutes. As with any tea, some prefer it stronger, some weaker. Strain into cups and add sugar or honey to taste. This is an old sore throat remedy in addition to being a refreshing drink.

Sassafras tea is also very good chilled on a hot summer day.

—DONNA STEVENSON

# SASSAFRAS TEA

*Sassafras*
The Herball

# Sauces, Relishes & Dressings

## YOGURT SALAD DRESSING

½ cup low fat yogurt
4 tbsp. salad oil
2 tbsp. cider vinegar
¼ tsp. curry (more if desired)
Optional: ¼ cup chopped nuts

Stir to blend; keep refrigerated; can be used with a variety of salads.

—ELEANOR B. GAMBEE

## AVOCADO CREAM

1 avocado, peeled and pit removed
⅔ cup sour cream
½ cup mayonnaise
2 tbsp. parsley, minced
1 tbsp. paprika
1 tbsp. onion, grated
1 small clove garlic, crushed
1 tbsp. lime juice
1 pinch cayenne pepper
salt and pepper to taste

Put all ingredients in a blender or food processor and blend until very smooth. Use as a dip or on fish, cold meats or salads.
*Yields 2 cups* —MRS. ROBERT CARLETON

## SHALLOT BUTTER

2 shallots, minced
juice of ½ lemon
¼ lb. butter

Cream ingredients together until light and fluffy and thoroughly blended. Spread on hot, grilled chicken or fish.

—MRS. E. W. PUGH, JR.

212.

1 cup chili sauce
1 cup mayonnaise
¼ cup Indian relish
1 hard boiled egg, chopped
½ tsp. chopped chives
¼ green pepper, chopped fine
1 tbsp. celery, chopped fine
½ tbsp. Dijon-style mustard
1 tsp. A-1 sauce
dash of paprika
coarsely ground black pepper

## COLD SAUCE FOR SHELLFISH

Mix together. Chill well and serve with shrimp, lobster or crabmeat.

—PHYL MALLORY

4 oranges
2 lemons
4 cups red currant jelly
½ cup vinegar
½ cup port
½ cup Marsala
2 tbsp. sugar
1 tbsp. Dijon-style mustard
salt and cayenne pepper to taste

## MOTHER'S CUMBERLAND SAUCE

Juice the citrus fruit and shred the peels finely. Simmer the peels for 5 minutes in plain water and drain. Combine the juices, drained peel, and other ingredients in a heavy pan and cook gently for 45 minutes. Bottle and seal. In Scotland we serve this sauce with game, cold turkey, ham and tongue.

Yields about 5 half pints

—MRS. FREDERIC P. HOUSTON

## ORANGE-LIME RELISH

2 large oranges
1 large lime
2 tbsp. white wine vinegar
2 tbsp. sugar (*or to taste*)
1 tbsp. minced scallion
salt to taste

Peel oranges and slice in a flat glass dish to catch all the juice. Slice the lime as thinly as possible. Combine with the other ingredients and chill very cold. Serve with any fat meat like ham or duck as an alternative to sweet fruits.

—JUDITH BECKWITH

## PESTO SAUCE

1 cup fresh basil leaves
2 tbsp. pine nuts
4 cloves garlic
¼ tsp. salt
½ cup olive oil

Place basil, pine nuts (raw sunflower seeds may be substituted), garlic and salt in the container of a blender. Turn on high speed and slowly pour in the oil. Continue blending until the sauce is pureed.

Pour sauce over 1 pound of pasta which has been cooked al dente and tossed with ½ stick of butter. Grind on fresh pepper.

*Serves 4*                                   —VIRGINIA CAPORALE

214.

1 cup Coleman's Dry Mustard
2 tbsp. flour
1 egg
1 pint vinegar
½ cup tarragon
½ cup basil
½ cup chives
2 garlic cloves

## HERB MUSTARD

Mix mustard, flour and egg in double boiler adding vinegar gradually. Stir and cook until mixture thickens. Add herbs which have been put through a grinder and cook for a minute longer.

—MRS. CHARLES BURLINGHAM

¼ cup sugar
1 tbsp. flour
2 tbsp. dry mustard
½ cup vinegar
1 or 2 eggs beaten with
1 cup milk

## MUSTARD SAUCE

Mix sugar, flour and mustard, blend with vinegar—place in top of double boiler over simmering water. Add egg mixture, cook while stirring until smoth and thickened.

—ELEANOR ISDALE

# SAUCE ITALIENNE

1 tbsp. minced scallion
2 tbsp. minced mushrooms
1 tbsp. olive oil
¾ cup Marsala
2 to 3 tomatoes, peeled, seeded, and chopped
½ cup rich brown gravy
½ cup diced ham
salt and pepper to taste
fresh parsley or basil

Wilt the scallion and mushrooms in the oil. Add the Marsala, tomatoes, and gravy and boil 4 to 5 minutes. Stir in the ham and season to taste. Pour over 1 pound of pasta, cooked al dente and tossed with a little good olive oil. Top with shredded parsley or basil.

*Serves 4*

—HANNAH M. RHODES

*Mushroom*
I discorsi

2½  cups fresh spinach leaves (lightly packed)
3    sprigs parsley
1    to 2 cloves garlic, chopped
salt and pepper to taste
¼    cup hot water
¼    cup olive oil
½    cup chopped walnuts
½    cup grated Parmesan

# SPINACH SAUCE

Wash and dry spinach leaves. Put leaves in blender with parsley, garlic, salt, pepper, oil, and water and puree until smooth. Remove the cover and push leaves down the sides until all are finely chopped. Add half the cheese. Add the walnuts and blend to chop them finely, but don't powder them. Pour sauce over cooked pasta lightly dressed with oil or over fish fillets before baking. Sprinkle on the remaining cheese. This sauce freezes well.

—EILEEN K. SCHOFIELD

*A Water to make the Breath Sweet*

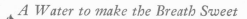

*Take the powder of Sage the powder of Winter Savery and the powder of Sweet marjerom the powder of cloves and mace a little nutmeg a little mufk fteep'd in the juice of lemons and white wine drink all thefe together a fpoonfull at a time evening and morning wᵗʰ the juice of lemons amongft it.*

—BOOK OF SIMPLES

# Cookies, Sweets & Desserts

# DUNDEE SOUFFLÉ

4  *egg whites*
3  *tbsp. sugar*
3  *tbsp. marmalade*
*Juice of half an orange*

Beat whites stiff, add sugar. Fold in orange juice and marmalade having mixed both together. Butter double boiler. Turn in mixture and place over boiling water. Steam for one hour or longer. Keep water simmering steadily, and do not remove cover until ready to serve. If a larger soufflé is needed, use 2 extra egg whites and other ingredients accordingly.

Sauce

3  *egg yolks well beaten*
¼  *cup powdered sugar*
¾  *cup of cream*
1  *tsp. vanilla*

Beat eggs and sugar together. Whip cream and mix lightly together, add vanilla and serve.

Sherry wine may be added in place of vanilla.

—CHARLOTTE HENCKEN

# GINGER SNAPS

¾   *cup butter*
¾   *cup sugar*
½   *cup molasses*
2½  *tsp. ground ginger*
1   *beaten egg*
1½  *cups flour*
1½  *tsp. brandy*

In a large saucepan heat and stir the butter, sugar, molasses and ginger until the butter melts. Cool and stir in the egg, and then the flour and brandy. Drop by teaspoonsful onto a greased cookie sheet. Bake at 350° about 15 minutes until edges start to brown. These are very thin and crisp.

*Yields 4 dozen*          —MRS. BURNHAM BOWDEN

# SOFT MOLASSES COOKIES

Cream the lard and brown sugar until fluffy. Add the egg and beat well. Dissolve the soda in the sour cream. Stir the sour cream and the molasses into the butter. Sift the flour, spices, and salt together, and gradually add to the liquids. When thoroughly blended stir in the raisins. Drop by teaspoonsful onto an oiled cookie sheet. Bake at 350° about 15 minutes until puffy and brown.

*Yields 2 dozen*          —MRS. C. E. ROCKWELL

½  *cup lard*
¼  *cup brown sugar*
1  *egg*
1  *tsp. baking soda*
½  *cup sour cream*
¾  *cup molasses*
2  *cups flour*
1  *tsp. cinnamon*
1  *tsp. ginger*
1  *tsp. salt*
1  *cup raisins*

# CYMBALLS

Dissolve soda in sour cream. Sift flour, mace, and salt together. Cream brown sugar and butter, add eggs, and beat well. Add sour cream and flour alternately to the creamed mixture and beat until well mixed. Stir in the vanilla and raisins. Drop by teaspoonsful onto a greased cookie sheet. Sprinkle with sugar. Bake at 350° approximately 15 minutes until puffy and brown.

*Yields 6 dozen cookies*     —MRS. C. E. ROCKWELL

¾  *cup sour cream*
1  *tsp. soda*
2  *cups flour*
1  *tsp. mace*
1  *tsp. salt*
½  *lb. light brown sugar*
¼  *lb. butter*
3  *eggs*
1  *tsp. vanilla*
¾  *cup raisins*
*sugar*

# SUGAR COOKIES

2 sticks butter
1 cup sugar
1 egg
1½ cups sifted cake flour
scant ½ tsp. salt
½ tsp. vanilla or almond
   extract
grated orange peel to taste

Cream butter and sugar till fluffy, and then beat in egg. Sift flour and salt together and then beat them into the batter in several additions. Add the flavoring extract. Drop by teaspoonfuls onto a lightly greased cookie sheet. Press flat with tines of a fork and sprinkle with orange peel. Bake at 375° for 12 to 15 minutes or until lightly browned. Let cookies cool on sheet a few minutes to harden before removing with a spatula. *Yields 4 dozen cookies*

—MRS. NILS ANDERSON, JR.

# HAZELNUT MACAROONS

⅔ cup sugar
3 egg whites
1 cup shelled hazelnuts

Stir the sugar into the unbeaten egg whites. Grate the hazelnuts (coarsely) and stir them into the egg white and sugar. Drop from a teaspoon onto a greased cookie sheet and bake at 325° about 30 minutes until cookies are browned on the surface.

*Yields 2 dozen*                    —MARIANNE BLOCK

*Filbert*
The Herball

222.

# HAZELNUT COOKIES

Mix all the ingredients together with your fingers until dough no longer sticks to the bowl. Divide into quarters. Using waxed paper, form each quarter into a roll 3" long and about 1½" in diameter. Refrigerate in the waxed paper overnight.

Cut in ¼" slices and bake on a well-greased cookie sheet 20 to 25 minutes at 350°. Cookies should be light brown.

4   oz. sweet butter at room temperature
1   cup and 2 tbsp. sifted, unbleached flour
2   tbsp. granulated sugar
1   egg yolk
⅔   cup freshly ground hazelnuts (filberts)

Coating:

Mix this thoroughly while cookies bake and put it on a plate. When cookies are done, quickly but gently lift them one at a time with a small spatula and turn them in the sugar to coat them. Cookies break easily. If they begin to stick to the cookie sheet, put them back in the oven just a minute. Store in the refrigerator.

1   pkg. (⅓ oz.) vanillin sugar
3   tbsp. confectioners sugar

—MRS. HAROLD G. BARKER

*For a Cold*

*Take a pint of milk boyle in it a large onion and at night when you go to bed take out your onion put thereto 2 or 3 ſpoonfulls of roſewater ſweeten it either with Sugar or honey of roſes & ſo drink it warme in your bed 3 nights together forbareing your ſupper thoſe nights you take it. probatum.*
—BOOK OF SIMPLES

# PECAN COINS

1 cup finely chopped pecans
1 cup sharp cheddar cheese, grated
1 cup sifted flour
½ cup or 1 stick butter
1 tsp. salt
⅛ tsp. pepper

Blend all ingredients (at room temperature) very thoroughly. Dough will be stiff—if necessary add 1 tablespoon milk. Divide dough in half and roll into two logs about the diameter of a quarter. Wrap well and chill. Slice ¼ inch thick and bake on a greased or Teflon coated pan in 350° oven for 10 to 12 minutes until lightly brown at the edges. Remove from pan and cool on rack.

These "coins" keep well on the shelf, indefinitely in the freezer, when well wrapped.

—BARBARA RIDGELY

# SESAME SEED COOKIES

½ cup sesame seeds
½ lb. butter
½ cup sugar
2 eggs
2½ cups flour
2 tsp. baking powder
pinch salt
saucer of milk

Toast the sesame seeds in an iron skillet on top of the stove or in the oven, stirring occasionally until they are golden. Cool.

Cream together the butter and sugar and beat in the eggs. Sift together the flour, baking powder, and salt, and work them into the butter mixture. Form the dough into a ball, wrap in waxed paper, and chill for 1 hour.

Pinch off pieces of dough and roll them in your hands into pencil shapes 2 inches long. Dip in milk and then in sesame seeds. Bake on an ungreased sheet for 20 minutes at 375°.

*Yields 48 cookies*

—VIRGINIA CAPORALE

# CRISP OATMEAL COOKIES

(Can be made with all brown sugar but the white makes them crispier. They will freeze but are hard to make in hurricane weather.)

Mix dry ingredients, egg and vanilla thoroughly. Melt butter and stir in. Drop from a teaspoon preferably onto a Teflon covered (otherwise a well buttered) cookie sheet. Bake in preheated 375° oven until edges are brown. These do not come off the cookie sheets well in bad weather.

Remove from sheets when cookies are set but still hot. If they get too brittle they may be reheated to get them off the cookie sheets.

*Yields approximately 10 dozen cookies*

—H. B. POST

½  lb. butter
1  egg
1  tsp. vanilla
1  cup granulated white sugar
1¼  cups brown sugar
2¼  cups oatmeal
5  tbsp. flour

# BOURBON BALLS

Beat the butter and salt together until butter is fluffy. Add the sugar and bourbon alternately. Beat well and add the nuts. Chill in the refrigerator until firm enough to handle. Remove and roll into small balls. Place on waxed paper in one layer in a pan and chill again. Dip in melted chocolate and chill in one layer until chocolate is set. Store in refrigerator.

*Yields 2 dozen*

—HOPE LEWIS FORD

½  lb. butter
1  lb. confectioners sugar
¼  cup good bourbon
1  cup finely chopped pecans
pinch of salt
4  oz. bitter chocolate

# GOOEY BROWNIES

4  square (oz.) bitter chocolate
⅔  cup butter
2  cups sugar
4  lightly beaten eggs
1  cup flour
1  cup chopped walnuts
1  tsp. vanilla
¼  tsp. salt

Melt chocolate and butter (carefully). Remove from heat, and add and stir in remaining ingredients. Bake in greased 9″ × 13″ pan in 350° oven 25 to 30 minutes.
Yields 36
—H. B. POST

# LEMON BARS

½  cup sifted powdered sugar
2  cups sifted flour
1  cup butter

## Crust

Sift the sugar and flour together and cut in the butter until the mixture will stick together. Press it into a 9 × 13 × 2 inch baking pan and bake at 350° about 20 minutes until lightly browned.

4  eggs
2  cups sugar
⅓  cup lemon juice
¼  cup flour
½  tsp. baking powder
powdered sugar and grated
   lemon rind

## Filling

Beat the eggs and then beat in the sugar and lemon juice. Sift the flour and baking powder into the egg mixture and beat well. Pour over the baked crust. Bake at 350° for 20 to 25 minutes until set. Sprinkle with powdered sugar and lemon rind.
Yields 18 bars
—HOPE LEWIS FORD

# SOUR CREAM HERMITS

Cream the butter and sugar. Beat in the eggs and sour cream. Sift the dry ingredients together and blend them well with the liquids. Add the raisins. Pour into a greased jelly roll pan or baking dish and bake 10 to 12 minutes at 375°. Cool and cut into squares.

*Yields 18 to 20* —MRS. LANGDON S. SIMONS

| | |
|---|---|
| ⅔ | cup butter |
| 2 | cups brown sugar |
| 2 | eggs |
| 1 | cup sour cream |
| 3½ | cups flour |
| 1 | tsp. baking soda |
| ½ | tsp. each cinnamon, cloves, and grated nutmeg |
| 1 | cup raisins |

# LEBKUCHEN

Beat eggs, then beat in sugar, fruit (chopped fine), and nuts. Sift in cinnamon, flour, baking powder, and salt, ad mix well. Pour into a greased jelly roll pan and spread to edges. Bake at 350° for 25 to 30 minutes until lightly browned. Remove from oven and cool slightly. Add lemon juice to confectioners sugar slowly until mixture becomes a thin icing. Spread over pastry and cut into 1 to 1½ inch squares while still warm.

*Yields 60 cookies* —GERDA SCHUYLER

| | |
|---|---|
| 4 | eggs |
| 1 | lb. dark brown sugar |
| 4 | oz. mixed, glazed fruit |
| ½ | cup chopped nuts |
| ½ | tsp. cinnamon |
| 2 | cups flour |
| 1 | tsp. baking powder |
| pinch salt | |
| 1 | cup confectioners sugar |
| 1 | to 2 tbsp. lemon juice |

# PINEAPPLE BARS

### Cake

2 cups sifted flour
2 cups sugar
½ tsp. salt
2 tsp. baking soda
1 (15 oz.) can crushed
  pineapple with juice
1 tsp. vanilla
2 eggs
1 cup chopped nuts

Stir first four ingredients together and then beat in the liquid ingredients in several additions. When mixture is smooth, beat in nuts. Pour into a greased jelly roll pan and bake at 325° for 25 to 30 minutes. The "cake" will pull away from the sides of the pan.

### Icing

1 stick butter
2 cups powdered sugar
1 tsp. vanilla
8 oz. cream cheese

Beat all ingredients together until the mixture is smooth. Frost the cooled "cake" and cut it into 2" square bars.
*Yields 48 bars*
—MRS. ERNEST STECKLEIN

# MOTHER'S FAMOUS PUMPKIN PIE

1 cup cooked and drained fresh
  pumpkin
2 eggs, lightly beaten
⅔ cup sugar
1 tsp. salt
1 tsp. ground ginger
1 tsp. grated nutmeg
1 cup scalded milk
1 cup heavy cream
1 unbaked 9-inch pie crust

Using an electric mixer at low speed, beat together the pumpkin, eggs, sugar, and spices until smooth. Gradually stir in by hand the milk and cream. Pour into an unbaked pie crust and bake at 400° for 5 minutes. Reduce heat to 350° and bake 45 minutes more or until a knife inserted in the center of the pie comes out clean.
*Yields 1 pie*
—ANN ROGENER

# PUMPKIN MOUSSE

In a metal measuring cup, sprinkle the gelatin over the rum to soften. Set the cup in a pan of simmering water and stir the rum until the gelatin is dissolved. In a large bowl beat the eggs, gradually adding the sugar until the eggs are very thick. Combine the pumpkin and spices and stir them into the eggs. Stir in the rum and blend well. Whip the cream and fold it into the pumpkin mixture. Pour into a soufflé dish or other serving bowl and chill several hours until set.
*Serves 6*

—EILEEN K. SCHOFIELD

1   *envelope unflavored gelatin*
¼   *cup rum*
4   *eggs*
⅔   *cup sugar*
1   *cup pureed pumpkin*
½   *tsp. cinnamon*
½   *tsp. ginger*
¼   *tsp. ground cloves*
¼   *tsp. mace*
1   *cup heavy cream*

# OKLAHOMA GREEN TOMATO PIE

Peel tomatoes and slice thickly. Place in a stainless steel or enameled saucepan with lemon juice and rind, salt and cinnamon. Simmer approximately ten minutes until tomatoes are barely tender. Mix sugar and cornstarch and stir into the tomato mixture. Continue cooking, stirring gently, until mixture is thickened and clear. Let mixture cool.

Line a 9″ pie plate with pastry and pour in cooled filling. Top with second crust and seal. Cut steam vents in the crust. Bake 40 to 50 minutes at 425°. This pie is delicious and the filling is kelly green.
*Yields 1 pie*

—MRS. DENNIS CANADA

8   *medium size green tomatoes*
2   *tbsp. lemon juice*
2   *tsp. lemon rind, grated*
½   *tsp. salt*
½   *tsp. cinnamon*
¾   *cup sugar*
2   *tbsp. cornstarch*
1   *tbsp. butter*
*pastry for 2-crust pie*

# PUMPKIN PUDDING

2    cups cooked pumpkin
½    cup light brown sugar
1    tbsp. molasses
½    cup sugar
1 ½  tsp. cinnamon
1 ½  tsp. ground ginger
dash of nutmeg
1    scant tsp. salt
1    tbsp. melted butter
3    eggs, well beaten
1    tbsp. brandy
2    cups heavy cream
½    cup sugar
3    tbsp. water

Mash cooked fresh or canned pumpkin and stir in brown sugar, molasses, and ½ cup granulated sugar. Beat well and then beat in the cinnamon, ginger, nutmeg, salt, butter and brandy. Beat well again and then beat in the eggs and, last of all, the cream.

In a small heavy metal saucepan dissolve the remaining ½ cup sugar in 3 tablespoons water and boil, swirling the pan until sugar caramelizes. Try to make a dark caramel without burning the sugar. Immediately pour the caramel into a warm 1 ½-quart glass baking dish and rotate the dish to coat the bottom. Cool to room temperature to allow caramel to set.

Pour the pudding on top of the caramel and bake at 325° for 50 minutes or until set. Remove from oven, cool, and refrigerate until ready to serve. To serve, turn out on a glass plate and let caramel run down the sides of the pudding. Pass kirsch and cream with the pudding so each person can add a few drops to his taste.

*Serves 6*

—PHYL MALLORY

*Pumpkin*
The Herball

# EGGNOG PIE

Separate eggs and reserve whites. In a double boiler combine yolks, ½ cup sugar, hot water and salt, and cook, stirring until the mixture coats wooden spoon. Meanwhile, soak the gelatin in the cold water for 5 minutes. Stir the gelatin mixture into the custard until it is completely dissolved.

Chill the custard. When it begins to set, fold in the egg whites, stiffly beaten, with the remaining ½ cup sugar and nutmeg. Add rum to taste. Pour into a baked pie shell and chill until firm. Whip the cream and spread it on top of the custard. Decorate with a little more nutmeg.

*Yields 1 pie*

—MRS. JOHN W. SANFORD

4   *eggs*
1   *cup sugar*
½   *cup hot water*
½   *tsp. salt*
¼   *cup cold water*
1   *envelope gelatin*
1   *tsp. grated nutmeg*
*rum to taste*
1   *baked pie shell*
¾   *cup heavy cream*

# SHIRKHAND (An East Indian Dessert)

Line a large colander with paper towels. Spread sour cream and yogurt on towels for 15 minutes to drain all excess water. Transfer to large bowl and mix. Stir in sugar and blend with a mixer or by hand until consistency is smooth. Add nutmeg, cardamom and saffron. May be served immediately or refrigerated for several days. A sumptuous dessert fit for a potentate.

*Serves 4*

—JOAN SIEBERT

8   *oz. sour cream*
8   *oz. plain yogurt*
1   *cup sugar*
½   *tsp. ground nutmeg*
*pinch of ground cardamom*
¼   *tsp. saffron*

*Cardamom*
The Herball

# PECAN TART

1    stick sweet butter
¾    cup sugar
salt to taste
2    eggs
2    tbsp. strong coffee
1⅓  cups pecans




6    tbsp. sweet butter
2    tbsp. vegetable shortening
1    cup sifted flour
½    tsp. salt
3    tbsp. ice water

Filling

Cut butter in chunks and place it in the container of a food processor with the sugar and salt. Blend them by turning on the processor 6 or 8 times. Add the rest of the ingredients and run the processor for 45 to 60 seconds until nuts are coarsely chopped. Don't powder them. Refrigerate filling until ready to use, then pour it into the prepared tart crust below and bake at 375° for 25 to 30 minutes until a knife inserted in the center comes out clean. Serve with whipped cream flavored with coffee or vanilla.

Short Pastry Crust

This pastry, made in a food processor, is very like real puff paste. Don't try to blend it as well as a regular pie crust.

Measure the butter and shortening. Cut them in pieces and place them in the freezer to become very cold. Place the flour and salt in the container of a food processor and flip it on once to mix. Add the very cold fat and flip on 6 or 8 times to cut it into coarse chunks. Pour the ice water through the feeder tube while turning on the processor and run it just until the chunks of butter are small, like grains of rice. Wrap the pastry in plastic wrap and refrigerate overnight, or at least half an hour.

Roll the dough out very thin and use it to line a 10- or 11-inch tart pan. Prick it with a fork, line it with foil filled with beans, and bake it at 425°

for 8 minutes. Remove the foil and beans and bake the crust 2 minutes more. Reduce oven heat to 375°, pour the filling in the crust, and bake as directed above.

*Serves 8*                           —MRS. GARDNER COWLES

# BLINTZ CASSEROLE

### Filling

If you can't find farmer cheese, use 1 lb. cream cheese plus 1 lb. creamed cottage cheese, drained. Mix all ingredients thoroughly and set aside.

| | |
|---|---|
| 2 | lbs. farmer cheese |
| 2 | eggs |
| ¼ | cup sugar |
| 1 | tbsp. lemon juice |
| dash salt | |

### Batter

When ready to bake, mix all batter ingredients in the order listed. Put half the batter in a greased 9 × 13-inch pan. Spread it evenly over the bottom, pour the filling on top and pat it out over the batter. Spread the remaining batter on top. (You may freeze the casserole at this point.) Bake at 350° for 1½ hours. Serve at room temperature or warm, with sour cream and cooked, tart, fruit on the side. I often use canned cherry pie filling.

*Serves 12*                          —BARBARA ROSENTHAL

| | |
|---|---|
| ½ | cup sugar |
| 1 | cup flour |
| 3 | tsp. baking powder |
| ¼ | cup milk |
| 1 | tsp. vanilla |
| 2 | eggs |
| 1½ | sticks butter, melted |

# APPLE-PECAN BAKE

4  large apples
2  eggs
1  cup chopped pecans
1  tsp. lemon juice
½  cup brown sugar
heavy cream

Core and mince the apples to make 4 cups full. Use tart, juicy apples and leave the peels on. Separate the egg yolks and mix them into the apples along with the nuts, lemon juice, and sugar. Beat the egg whites stiff and fold them into the apple mixture.

Pour into a buttered, flat baking dish. Set the dish in a pan of hot water. Bake at 350° for 45 minutes or until a tester comes out clean. Serve hot or warm with heavy cream or whipped cream.

*Serves 4 to 6*
—LIZA FOSBURGH

# RASPBERRY SOUFFLÉ

6  egg whites
½  cup milk
1  tbsp. cornstarch
3  tbsp. granulated sugar
1  tsp. vanilla extract
1  lb. raspberries (*best fresh*)
¼  cup heavy cream

Preheat oven to 425° and butter your soufflé dish. In a small, heavy saucepan, stir the milk into the cornstarch until it is smooth, then add the sugar and vanilla. Stir constantly over gentle heat until mixture thickens. Remove from heat and let cool. Stir in the cream. When mixture reaches room temperature, stir it into the raspberries and then fold in the stiffly beaten egg whites. Pour into the buttered dish and bake at 425° for 20 to 25 minutes until soufflé is puffed and browned. Serve immediately.

*Yields 1 soufflé*
—MRS. HENRY E. COE III

# CRISP-TOPPED FRUIT COBBLER

Toss fresh or frozen blueberries, raspberries, blackberries, or sliced peaches with the lemon juice. Mix ½ cup sugar with the cornstarch and ¼ teaspoon salt. Sprinkle this over the fruit and mix it well. Butter an 8-inch square baking dish with 1 tablespoon of butter and spread the fruit mixture evenly in it.

Cream together the remaining 3 tablespoons of butter and ¾ cup of the sugar. Sift the flour, baking powder and salt together and add it alternately with the milk. Spread this batter over the fruit leaving ½-inch clearance between the batter and the dish. Sprinkle the remaining ½ cup sugar on the batter and pour the boiling water evenly over it. If the fruit was frozen in syrup, decrease the amount of water by ¼ to ½ cup. Bake at 350° one hour until crust is browned and very crisp. Serve warm or at room temperature with whipped cream or ice cream.

*Serves 8*

—MRS. JOHN W. SANFORD

| 2 | cups fruit |
|---|---|
| juice ½ lemon | |
| 1 ¾ | cups sugar |
| 1 | tbsp. cornstarch |
| ½ | tsp. salt |
| 4 | tbsp. butter |
| ½ | cup milk |
| 1 | cup sifted flour |
| 1 | tsp. baking powder |
| 1 | cup boiling water |

*Peach*
The Herball

# PERSIMMON PUDDING

2½  cups fresh persimmon pulp
     from very ripe fruits
1  cup brown sugar
2  eggs
dash of salt
2  cups flour
2  tsp. vanilla
⅔  cup buttermilk
1  tsp. baking soda
1  to 2 cups pecans

In a large bowl beat eggs lightly, add sugar, pulp, spices and salt. Mix and add buttermilk with soda. Finally add flour. Mix well (no need to beat).

Grease a baking pan. (An 8 × 8 × 2 pan results in a more pudding-like texture. A larger pan results in a pastry-like texture). Pour mixture in pan. Cover with pecans and bake 45 minutes at 350°.

*Serves 6*

—DAPHNE BALICK

# POACHED PEARS WITH CARAMEL SAUCE

4  pears, ripe, but firm
2½  cups sugar
2½  cups water
2  inch strip lemon peel,
    ½ inch wide
2  tbsp. vanilla

Pare, halve and core pears. Combine other ingredients and bring to boiling, reduce heat and simmer 10 minutes or until tender, testing with a needle. Allow to cool in the liquid. Drain pears on a wire cake rack and chill. (Reserve poaching liquid for more fruit poaching.)

Sauce

1  cup pear poaching liquid
1  cup heavy cream

Simmer poaching liquid in small saucepan until syrup is reduced by half. Add cream and continue cooking until sauce is golden and coats a spoon. Serves 2 pear halves per person with sauce. Whipped cream may be added to top.

*Serves 4*

—MRS. GRAYSON L. KIRK

# POACHED FRUIT

In a large saucepan heat the first 5 ingredients together, stirring, until sugar dissolves. Add the fruit, and if it is not covered by the wine, add enough water to cover it. Simmer gently until the fruit is tender all the way to the center. Remove the fruit to a serving dish and boil the poaching liquid until it is reduced to 2 cups. Pour the syrup over the fruit. Serve at room temperature with unsweetened whipped cream.

*Serves 8*                    —SHAREN BENENSON

| | |
|---|---|
| 2 | cups sugar |
| 1 | bottle dry red wine |
| ½ | tsp. ground cinnamon |
| ½ | tsp. ground cloves |
| ½ | tsp. grated nutmeg |
| 8 | peeled pears or seedless oranges or a pineapple peeled, cored and cut in 8 pieces |

# CHESTNUTS IN SYRUP

Slit shells of fresh chestnuts in three or four places, drop in boiling water for 5 minutes, and peel and skin while still warm. Cover dried nuts with boiling water, and when cool enough to handle, slip off brown skins. Place the nuts in a heavy saucepan and cover with water. Add the rest of the ingredients and stir to mix. You may substitute fruit brandy or a cordial for the sherry. Cover, bring to a boil, and simmer until done. This may take 3 to 4 hours if dried nuts are used. A cooked chestnut, cut in half, will have the same chewy texture and light caramel color throughout. The center shouldn't look powdery. Add water during cooking if necessary to keep pan from becoming dry.

Serve at room temperature over vanilla ice cream, just plain, or with whipped cream on the side.

*Serves 6*                    —B. ELIZABETH WUNDER

| | |
|---|---|
| 1½ | lbs. fresh chestnuts |
| ¾ | lb. dried chestnuts |
| water | |
| 1 | lemon |
| 1 | tbsp. anise seeds |
| ½ | cup raisins |
| ½ | cup sherry |

# QUINCE COMPOTE

6  ripe Quinces
water
¾  cup sugar

Quarter, core and pare the quinces. Halve the quarters and place in baking dish. Cover with sugar and set aside. Cover the cores, seeds and skins with hot water and boil ½ hour. Strain the juice over the quince slices. Cover pan and bake about two hours in 300° oven, until slices turn a glorious deep pink color and are tender. Delectable served chilled as a fruit dessert, or as a topping for ice cream.

*Serves 6*

—ELIZABETH P. CORNING

# BLACK FRUIT CAKE - 1821

4   lbs. currants
3   lbs. raisins
½   lb. sugar
1   lb. butter
1   lb. flour
10  eggs
3   nutmegs, grated
1   glass brandy
ground cloves and cinnamon
    to taste

Cream butter and sugar. Add eggs, one at a time, and beat until well blended. Add brandy and blend mixture. Sift flour with seasonings and add slowly stirring well. Fold in currants and raisins.

Bake in 3 buttered and floured loaf pans in a moderate oven—350°—about 1 hour or until toothpick comes out clean. For storage, soak cheese cloth in brandy, wrap cake in cloth, wax paper and foil. Place in an air tight container. May also be frozen very successfully.

*Yields 3 cakes*

—MRS. C. E. ROCKWELL

# BEST ORANGE CAKE

Cream butter and sugar and add yolks. Beat until thick and lemon colored. Sift dry ingredients together and add alternately with the orange juice. Fold in stiffly beaten egg whites. Bake in two greased and floured pans in a moderate oven (350°) for 20 minutes. Turn out of pans to cool to room temperature. When cold, spread orange filling between layers and frost with orange frosting.

| | |
|---|---|
| 4 | tbsp. butter |
| 1 | cup sugar |
| 2 | eggs, separated |
| 1½ | cups cake flour |
| 2 | tsp. baking powder |
| pinch salt | |
| ½ | cup orange juice |

## Filling

Mix sugar, cornstarch and salt. Gradually add water, rind, juice, and egg yolk. Cook in double boiler until smooth and thick. Fold in butter and pineapple. Cool before spreading between layers.

| | |
|---|---|
| 6 | tbsp. sugar |
| 1½ | tbsp. cornstarch |
| pinch of salt | |
| ½ | cup water |
| ½ | tsp. grated orange rind |
| ½ | cup orange juice |
| 1 | egg yolk, slightly beaten |
| 1 | tbsp. butter |
| ½ | cup crushed pineapple |

## Orange Icing

Bring orange juice and rind to a boil; strain and put as much hot juice over sugar as needed to make the proper consistency for spreading. Add rum, sherry or whiskey.

*Yields 1 cake*

| | |
|---|---|
| Juice of 1 orange | |
| 1 | orange rind grated |
| 1½ | cups confectioner's sugar |
| 1 | tsp. rum |

—PHYL MALLORY

# POPPY SEED CAKE

⅓    cup poppy seed
2    cups buttermilk
2    tsp. vanilla
1    cup butter (2 sticks)
1½    cups sugar
4    eggs
2½    cups sifted flour
4    tsp. baking powder
2    tsp. baking soda
1    tsp. salt
cookie crumbs or flour
⅓    cup sugar
1    tsp. cinnamon

Stir the first three ingredients together and let stand overnight. Next day cream together the butter and sugar, then beat in one egg at a time. Sift the flour, baking powder, soda, and salt together and add to the eggs and butter alternately with the poppy seed mixture.

Grease a tube pan and dust it with cookie crumbs or flour. Pour in half the batter. Mix the ⅓ cup sugar and cinnamon and sprinkle half of it on the batter in the pan. Pour in the remaining batter and sprinkle with the remaining cinnamon-sugar. Bake at 350° for 40 minutes to 1 hour until a tester comes out clean. This cake freezes well and is excellent sliced, toasted, and buttered also. *Yields 1 tube cake*    —EMILY FORD COX

# OLD FASHIONED WINE JELLY

½    cup sugar
½    cup water
1    pkg. gelatin
1    cup orange, lemon, or lime juice
½    cup red wine
grated peel of 1 orange

In an enameled saucepan mix the sugar and gelatin with the water and let stand to soften. Add the juice (ideally a mixture of the three), wine, and peel, and heat and stir until gelatin is dissolved. Do not boil. Pour into glasses and chill. *Serves 4*    —MRS. DONALD STRAUS

# APPLE RAISIN CAKE

Mix dry ingredients in a large bowl. Beat in the mayonnaise, milk and eggs and continue beating at low speed for 2 minutes. Scrape bowl frequently. Stir in apples, raisins and nuts. Divide batter between two greased and floured 8-inch, round baking pans. Bake at 350° for 45 minutes. Cool in pans for 10 minutes before turning out on racks to cool completely. Fill and frost with whipped cream.

*Yields 1 cake*

—ANN BROOKS

| | |
|---|---|
| 3 | cups unsifted flour |
| 2 | cups sugar |
| 2 | tsp. baking soda |
| 1½ | tsp. cinnamon |
| ½ | tsp. nutmeg |
| ½ | tsp. salt |
| ¼ | tsp. clove |
| 1 | cup mayonnaise |
| ⅓ | cup milk |
| 2 | eggs |
| 3 | cups peeled, chopped apples |
| 1 | cup raisins |
| ½ | cup chopped walnuts |
| 2 | cups heavy cream, whipped |

# COLD LEMON SOUFFLÉ

Put the egg yolks, 1 cup of the sugar, the lemon juice and rind in a large saucepan and whisk over low heat until mousse-like. Taste to see if the additional ½ cup of sugar is needed. Remove from heat and beat until cool. Add the cream whipped softly so that it barely holds its shape. Melt the gelatin over low heat and add it. Stir the mousse over ice until thickened and then fold in the egg whites, beaten stiff but not dry. Turn into a collared soufflé case and put in the refrigerator. When it is firm, press crumbs on upstanding edge and decorate with whipped cream and nuts.

*Yields 1 soufflé*

—BARBARA ROSENTHAL

| | |
|---|---|
| 6 | large eggs separated |
| 1½ | cups sugar |
| ⅔ | cup lemon juice |
| | Grated lemon rind |
| 2 | cups heavy cream |
| 2 | tbsp. gelatin in ½ cup cold water |
| 1 | extra egg white |

*Preserves*

# MINT SAUCE

*Sterilize 4 one pint jars*
*2 cups mint leaves, chopped*
*3 cups vinegar*
*6 cups sugar*

Boil vinegar and sugar together until it becomes as syrupy as good maple syrup, about ½ hour. Fill jars one quarter full of finely chopped mint leaves, pour on hot syrup and seal.

Mint leaves may be any variety, and can be chopped in a blender with small amount of water.

Easy and delicious with lamb. Keeps well in refrigerator after opening. May be thinned with water if too sugary. Serve warm.
*Yields 4 pints*                                    —ELEANOR B. BELL


# BEET PICKLES

*About 15 lbs. beets*
*4½  cups cider vinegar*
*3     cups sugar*
*6     cardamom pods*
*1     stick cinnamon*
*2     tbsp. mustard seed*
*2     tbsp. coriander seed*
*½    tbsp. whole cloves*
*½    tbsp. whole allspice*
*½    tbsp. black peppercorns*
*½    tbsp. celery seed*
*scant tbsp. turmeric*
*1     cup water*

Simmer beets in a large pot of water until they are just tender. Slip the skins off under cold running water. Slice beets in ¼ inch slices. Meanwhile, combine the vinegar, sugar, and spices in another deep pot and simmer ½ hour. Add the 1 cup of water and the beets, bring to a boil, and cook 1 minute. Pack the beets into hot pint jars, one jar at a time. (I heat the jars to 225° in the oven.) Add enough liquid to raise the contents to the bottom of the jar's neck. Seal with a warm, boiled, dome lid. Store at least 2 weeks before serving. These are my favorite "last minute" vegetable.
*Yields 7 or 8 pints*                               —SHAREN BENENSON

# MOCK WATERMELON PICKLE

Use cucumbers which have started to turn yellow. Peel and seed them and cut them into pieces about 1 inch long and ½ inch thick. Place them in a deep pot. Dissolve the alum in the water and add to the cucumbers. Heat slowly to boiling, remove from the stove, and let stand in a warm place for 2 hours. Pour off alum water and chill cucumbers in ice water.

Heat the vinegar and sugar together until the sugar melts. Tie the spices in a bag. Add them to the syrup, and boil 5 minutes. **Drain the** cucumbers. Place them in a jar or crock, and pour the syrup over, leaving out the spice bag. On the next 3 successive mornings, drain off the syrup and boil it for 2 minutes with the spice bag. On the first 2 mornings, return the hot syrup to the cucumber crock. On the third, add the cucumbers to the boiling syrup. Cook long enough to heat the cucumbers through (1 or 2 minutes after syrup returns to a boil), pack into hot jars, and seal.

The white rind of watermelons has been virtually eliminated in hybrids now available. This receipt is an acceptable substitute for those of us who are addicted to watermelon pickles.
*Yields about 6 pints*                              —LUCY STALEY

5 *large, mature, cucumbers*
2 *tbsp. alum*
4 *quarts water*
4 *cups sugar*
2 *cups cider vinegar*
2 *tbsp. whole cloves*
2 *sticks cinnamon*

*Clove*
Hortus Sanitatis

# DILL PICKLE CHIPS

½  bushel small cucumbers
large bunch dill
8  cloves garlic
1  quart cider vinegar
3  quarts water
½  cup salt

Wash and slice enough cucumbers to fill loosely 8 quart jars. Add 1 or 2 dill heads and part of a dill stalk to each jar along with a large garlic clove. Bring the water, vinegar, and salt to a boil and pour it over the cucumbers. Seal the jars. Store at least 1 week before serving.

*Yields 8 quarts*                    —MRS. LEWIS F. CAMP


# PICKLED MUSHROOMS

1  lb. fresh mushrooms
4  scallions, finely chopped
3  tbsp. dry sherry
3  tbsp. lemon juice
2  tbsp. sugar
1  tbsp. soy sauce
1  tsp. salt
dash monosodium glutamate

Slice the mushroom caps ⅜ inch thick. Broil in one layer until lightly browned. Combine the remaining ingredients and simmer for 5 minutes. Add the mushrooms, bring to a boil, and seal in a pint jar or cool and freeze. Serve chilled after storing at least 1 day.

*Yields about 1 pint*                    —SYLVIA STEIN

# BREAD AND BUTTER PICKLES

Wash cucumbers and slice paper thin. Slice onions and chop peppers. Combine cucumbers, onion and peppers and add salt. Let stand for 3 hours. Drain *thoroughly*. Combine vinegar, sugar and spices in large kettle. Bring to a boil. Add the vegetables. Heat thoroughly but do not boil. Pack while hot in sterilized jars.

Celery seed, a sprig of fresh dill or dried dill seeds may also be used.

*Yields 4 pints*                    —DOROTHY GREENLEE

25  *or so medium cucumbers*
8   *large white onions*
2   *large sweet green peppers*
½   *cup pickling salt*
5   *cups cider vinegar*
5   *cups sugar (2½ lbs.) or same amount light brown sugar*
2   *tbsp. whole mustard seed*
1   *tsp. ground cloves*
½   *tsp. ground turmeric*

# TOMATO MARMALADE

Dip tomatoes into boiling water one minute and skin and cut into chunks. Strain and measure juice, discard half. Combine remaining juice with tomatoes, measure and put into large kettle. Add one cup sugar for each cup of tomatoes and juice. Add slivered fruit and spices. Bring to a boil, lower heat and cook slowly until thick, stirring constantly when it begins to thicken. Pour into hot sterile jars and seal. Sweet and spicy—a great meat or fowl accompaniment.

*Yields 5 half-pints*                    —SARA CARTER

8   *lbs. tomatoes, skinned and cut into chunks*
3   *oranges, unpeeled, sliced thin and cut into slivers*
2   *lemons, unpeeled, sliced thin and cut into slivers*
8   *sticks cinnamon bark*
1   *tbsp. whole cloves*
*Sugar—one cup for each of prepared tomatoes*

# STRAWBERRY PRESERVE MADE IN THE SUN

20 quarts of fresh strawberries hulled, not washed
20 lbs. granulated sugar
2 quarts of rhubarb cut up

Place strawberries in two large kettles, putting 10 quarts of berries in each. Add just enough water—a very small amount—to keep strawberries from scorching. Boil the strawberries for 20 minutes slowly.

Cook the rhubarb in a separate kettle.

Heat the sugar, 10 lbs. each, in pans in oven. After the strawberries have cooked, remove from stove and add the heated sugar. Add rhubarb. Boil the mixture 3 minutes.

Set up a table on the lawn. Place the strawberries, when cool, on platters on the table with glass underneath and cover with glass (storm windows are excellent for cover). Leave the strawberries outside for 2 days if it is sunny, or longer, until they have reached the desired consistency for a preserve.

Place extra protection over strawberries at night.

Stir once a day.

When the preserve is finished, bring inside the house and put in jars and cover with paraffin.

The same recipe can be used in the peach season with fresh peaches.

*Yields about 24 pints*

—MRS. W. LEICESTER VAN LEER

*Strawberry*
The Herball

# JELLY OF ROSE HIPS

Wash and trim rose hips and weigh them. Put hips in a deep kettle and add 1 cup of water for each pound of hips. Simmer until fruit is tender and pass the pulp through a fine sieve to remove the seeds. Weigh the pulp and add one pound of sugar for each pound of pulp. (Or measure it and add equal measure.) Boil the mixture until it sheets from a wooden spoon. Pour into hot jars and seal.

—MRS. MORTIMER J. FOX

*Rose hips which have been touched by frost*
*water*
*sugar*

# GREEN PEPPER JELLY

Place the ground peppers in a large kettle. You may substitute 3 to 4 tablespoons hot pepper flakes for the fresh ground if you cannot handle them. Cover with the sugar and vinegar, bring to a rolling boil, and cook 1 minute, stirring constantly. Pour through a fine sieve and let stand for 1 minute. Skim off the skin.

Bring the mixture to a boil again and add the pectin. Add green food coloring or a little ground hot pepper for decoration. Skim, and pour into hot, sterile ½ pint jars. Seal. This is delicious served with cheese and crackers.
*Yields 8 half-pints*          —MRS. F. DAVID LAPHAM

| | |
|---|---|
| 3 | *small, hot red peppers, seeded and ground* |
| 3 | *large green peppers, seeded and ground* |
| 6½ | *cups sugar* |
| 1½ | *cups cider vinegar* |
| 1 | *bottle fruit pectin* |
| | *green food coloring or more red pepper* |

# SOME NOTES ABOUT THE ILLUSTRATIONS

To those who question the wisdom of illustrating a 20th century book with line-cuts (woodcuts and engravings) from the 16th and 17th centuries a few words of explanation are due. It may be surprising that such a variety of foodstuffs, many of animal origin, should ever have been encountered in botanical books. The case is, however, that one class of botanical works, the herbals, was really medical in its intention, and had to include medicaments from all three kingdoms of nature, although plants provided most of the medicines. What is more dietary precepts were part and parcel of medical practice since the body was perceived as being continually in danger of imbalance from too much or too little heat, cold, dryness, or moisture, and any such imbalance was thought to result in harm to the body's well-being, and foods, which all possessed these qualities in varying degrees and combinations, were of constant concern to the physician in the course of administering a cure. Hence, there was an abundance of illustrations of herbs, spices, vegetables, meats, bread, and drink in most of the early herbals, often incorporated into genrescenes that showed their preparation or use. It is from that rich repertoire that these pictures from the collection of The New York Botanical Garden have been drawn. Since they also came from the period when the foundations of modern cuisine and cookery were being established they add an extra historical dimension to this publication.

The earliest illustrations come from a 1511 Venetian edition of the *Hortus Sanitatis*, the Latin for Garden of Health. Originally published in the city of Mainz in 1491 its pictures have a thoroughly Germanic style, particularly in the matter of cos-

Hortus Sanitatis

tumes, which have been adapted here to suit the Venetian taste. All the drawings are anonymous, as is so often the case with early books, and the text is an anonymous compilation as well, consisting of extracts from Pliny, Dioscorides, Avicenna, and numerous other sources.

Others works, in descending order of age, are as follows:

The *Kreuterbuch* (Plantbook) of Eucharius Roeslin, 1540, Frankfort on Main, with woodcuts attributed to Hans Beham.

Dioscorides' *De medicinali materia libri sex* (Of Medicinal Materials in Six Books) as translated from Greek into Latin by Jean Ruel, 1549 at Frankfort. The first illustrated Dioscorides to be printed, with woodcuts attributed to Hans Beham.

*Commentarii in libros sex* (Commentaries in Six Books) on Dioscorides by Pier Andrea Mattioli, 1554, Venice. Contains 562 small woodcuts by anonymous Italian artists.

*De tuenda bona valetudine* (Of Preserving Good Health) by Helius Eobanus Hessus, 1560, Frankfort. Woodcuts attributed to Hans Beham and Hans Weiditz.

*I discorsi* (The Discourses) on Dioscorides by Pier Andrea Mattioli, 1563, Venice. This Italian translation of Mattioli's work contains large woodcuts by Giorgio Liberale, the artist, and Wolfgang Meyerpeck, who cut the blocks.

The *Kreuterbuch* (Plantbook) of Adam Lonitzer, 1577, Frankfort. This is a revised edition of Roeslin's *Kreuterbuch* with additional woodcuts attributed to Hans Beham and Hans Weiditz. The book and its illustrations continued to be printed until 1783!

*De plantis epitome utilissima* (A Condensed Version of the Most Useful Plants) by Pier Andrea Mattioli, 1586, Frankfort on Main, with small woodcuts. This was an abridged edition of Mattioli's work done under a German editor.

The *Kreuterbuch* (Plantbook) of Hieronymus Bock, 1587, Strassburg, woodcuts by David Kandel. A late edition of this popular book which first appeared in 1539 without any illustrations.

*The Herball* of John Gerard, edited by Thomas Johnson, London, 1633. This edition corrects numerous errors in the text and the captions to the illustrations. The latter are woodcuts originally produced for the *Neuw Kreuterbuch* of Jacob Dietrich von Bergzabern (Jacobus Theodorus Tabernaemontanus) by German artists, plus others from the Plantin Press of Antwerp by Flemish craftsmen.

*The Theatrum Botanicum* (Theatre of Plants) by John Parkinson, London, 1640, woodcuts by anonymous English artists.

*Flora Danica* (The Danish Flora) by Simon Paulli, Copenhagen, 1647. The illustrations are woodcuts commissioned for this book. Paulli was the first Royal Physician of Denmark.

*Histoire Generale des Drogues* (The General History of Drugs) by Pierre Pomet, Paris, 1694. Illustrated with engravings. Pomet was chief apothecary to Louis XIV of France.

The titles of the books and the occupations of the authors demonstrate the affinity of botany, pharmacy, and nutrition. We hope that this book will provide a good tonic for your culinary bookshelf, and will guide you to a gourmet's paradise.

—FRANK J. ANDERSON
*Hon. Curator of Rare Books and Mss.*
*Library of the New York Botanical Garden*

# Index

*Lily*

De plantis epitome utilissima

Kreuterbuch (Lonitzer)

255.

# ACKNOWLEDGMENTS

I want to thank all of those who have contributed to this book. The names of those whose recipes are included appear with the recipes, but countless others have helped. Dorothy Collins typed and retyped the manuscript, correcting the spelling and punctuation every time. Barbara Cusack has attended to a year and a half's daily details.

Jules Bond has advised us at each step toward publication. Holland Vose Brigham's selection of illustrations from the NYBG Library and her artistic advice have given the book the character we hoped for. Frank Anderson, who is familiar with every book in the Rare Book Room, directed us to our illustrations, and Lothian Lynas, Rose Li, and Gerard McKiernan of the Library staff were extremely helpful. Terry Slater and Mary Homans of our Cookbook Committee found and documented the illustrations.

Other members of the Garden Council's Cookbook Committee who solicited recipes, contributed their own, and gave hours of consideration and advice to this project were Faith McCurdy, Barbara Rosenthal, Dorothy Greenlee, and Jane Bancroft. We also had a group of dedicated recipe testers. Peg Bowden, Phyllis Young, Happy Post, Penny Coe, Cathy Riley, Dorothy Steere, Laura Bishop, Do Clarke, Alice Nolan and Jennifer Stewart have baked, simmered, and sautéed valiantly in our cause. All of the above and many others have provided the inspiration necessary to complete this book. —SHAREN BENENSON

Hortus Sanitatis